TO BE A DRESSAGE RIDER

JANE KIDD

First published in 2007 by
The Pony Club
Stoneleigh Park
Kenilworth
Warwickshire
CV8 2RW

Produced for the Pony Club by Barbara Cooper
Designed by Nancy Lawrence
Line drawings:
pages 11, 38, 58 and 60: Gisela Holstein
pages 36, 37, 68, 69, 70 and 79: Maggie Raynor
Frontispiece photograph: Kevin Sparrow
Other photographs: Jane Kidd

ISBN-10: 0-954 8863-8-0
ISBN-13: 978-0-954 8863-8-7

British Cataloguing in Publication Data available
on request.

CONTENTS

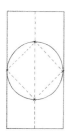

This picture conveys that sense of eagerness from the horse, a showing off of his natural ability with elastic, expressive steps—key parts of good dressage. Dressage is the pursuit of perfection which is rarely, if ever, achieved and in this and many of the following pictures there are faults that are easy to focus on. In this case, for example, you will note that the contact is loose and the curb rein tighter than the snaffle. However, a principle that I follow as closely as possible in this book is that you can learn more by looking at the positives (e.g. eagerness and elasticity) than by criticising the negatives.

INTRODUCTION

To be a dressage rider—that is what so many want to be. Some want to improve scores in eventing, or to teach the horse to be more balanced and athletic so that he jumps and generally goes better. Some want the challenge of facing a judge at the end of the centre line, to test whether their training has been worthwhile and they can score higher than others.

It's a demanding journey being a dressage rider—you are aiming for harmony with the horse, and that means understanding his mind, keeping in balance with and ultimately influencing his movement. However, the fantastic thing about dressage is that the start point is very easy. If you can get a horse to stop, that is the first step towards doing all those exotic movements like piaffe and passage. Everybody can find a level where they can compete in dressage, whether it is the walk/trot test for the Pony Club, the Preliminary or Training level for Affiliated Dressage, the Intro tests for Eventing, or Grand Prix for the very talented and serious. What is more, there are plenty of people who do not want to compete but just to enjoy training at home. Nearly every rider can find an area of dressage that is within their capabilities but still a challenge.

WHAT IS DRESSAGE?

The first stage is to really understand what dressage means. Of course the horse has to be obedient—but this is not achieved by making him dour and subservient; it is about bringing out your horse's natural ability: the way he moves when free and excited in the fields. Then, when sitting on him, being able to get him to do that same free movement whenever you ask him. In other words, you are developing and controlling his natural gymnastic ability. This is what makes dressage exciting and will make your horse a better jumper and a more eye-catching mover.

Not all horses are brilliant movers: some are old and stiff, some have breeding that limits their scope, but it is their natural ability that dressage riders are responsible for bringing out, maintaining, and teaching them to do movements without spoiling it. The international authority for the sport, the FEI, name their objective as 'the Happy Athlete'.

READ IT AGAIN, AND AGAIN, AND AGAIN.

To make your horse a Happy Athlete the two most important chapters in this book are *The Fundamentals for the Rider* and *The Fundamentals for the Horse*. The ideas in these chapters are quite straightforward but need returning to again and again. Keep your dressage simple and really master these basics so that they become natural and automatic to you. It is amazing how much easier your horse will find his work if you learn to stretch, lengthen and allow, and how much more of an exhilarating ride he will be if you keep returning to the Training Scales. Just because the goals are simple, however, does not mean that they are easy to achieve. It takes time, persistence, and dedication to truly establish them, but keep on the straight path towards them and avoid the diversions!

BASICS

I have looked at becoming a dressage rider from the perspective of training first the rider then the horse. Some of the most important topics are looked at in both parts and I am not going to apologise for what at first sight might appear like repetition. Looking at these key topics for a second time in a different way will, I hope, add depth to your understanding rather than tedium from a lack of novelty. They are topics that you will have to deal with over and over again and although simple to name, very tough to master. The more time you spend on the basics and the less on skipping through to the more advanced movements, the greater will be your rewards as a rider able to work in harmony with the horse.

HORSES AND PONIES

Sorry, pony riders—as ponies are horses, but horses are not ponies, I have referred to horses throughout this book, though it covers both ponies and horses.

THE PICTURES

I have tried to use pictures with which everybody can associate. Some of the riders are talented and successful, others have never won a dressage class. Most are pretty young but although the material in this book is aimed at Pony Club riders, now under 25 years, it applies to anyone of any age, so some are more mature.

My thanks go to the riders who illustrated both the good and upon request, what was pretty foreign to them, the bad! My special thanks to Nathalie Allen, Danielle Dunn, Ella and Tom McEwen, Thomas Windsor-Clive, Olivia Kuropatwa, Carole Farmar, and Izzy, Asher and Merri Mayers. I thank also Islay Auty, chairman of British Dressage's BYRDS who read the section on the rider, Jenny Iles my Pilates teacher who helped me tackle core stability, and to Merri Mayers who did so much checking and correcting.

The youngest rider, 17 year-old Asher Mayers-Thompson, wrote a poem that captures some of the youthful vigour that is so important for the sport.

TO BE A DRESSAGE RIDER

To help my pony be very happy,
I must not be grabby and slappy,
If I get him in front of the leg,
Then I will not have to beg.
I must do my very best,
To get my pony on the road to success.

To help my pony trot his best,
To help my pony through his test,
To make my pony supple and through,
Then he can do what he should do.
And if my pony is very good,
I will have done just what I should.

It is my real pleasure to work with able young riders like these who have helped me. I hope this book will make many more youngsters realise their talent is all too often hidden behind an incorrect approach towards dressage and that this book will lead to many more happy athletes in the dressage arenas.

CHAPTER 1
THE FUNDAMENTALS

This is the most important chapter in the whole book. To get value from it don't just read it once, but keep on re-reading it and making sure you have got the hang of what is said and can put it into practice. Then, when you go on to the rest of the book, keep returning to these basics and check that you are *still* putting them into practice. You will be repaid a hundredfold if you do this. Your horse will go better and better because he is carrying a balanced load and he can understand your precisely-given commands.

Dressage can be made pretty complicated, but to me there are three fundamentals for the rider. If whenever people rode they began by checking these fundamentals, we would have many more good riders, and many happier horses.

- The first is the upward stretching–the body is upright and poised.
- The second is the downward lengthening– letting the legs fall towards the ground.
- The third is the allowing hands–letting go of the shoulders, arms and wrists.

Of course there is a lot more involved in developing a good position, but these are the basics and if you work on getting the stretch, lengthening and allowing, you will soon be riding in a much better balance. The problem is that we riders are so keen to progress and this seems pretty straightforward so we say: 'yes I can do that', and leap on to the next stage.

When you are thinking about this you might be able to stretch your spine upwards, but it has to become automatic, and it must be kept upright all the time.

Kyra Kyrklund, one of the greatest dressage riders and trainers in the world today, says that you have to do an action 100,000 times before it becomes automatic; if you are correcting a mistake 5,000 times the right way before starting the 100,000. So when you get on your horse go through this check list, and even if and when you are riding a Grand Prix horse it would still be a good idea to do so.

Kyra Kyrklund, one of the world's great riders and trainers, who has explained why so much work is needed to correct a mistake.

Make your own check list and put it in the tack room, or keep it in your mind every time you get on a horse. I have noted down the essentials, but you might add points that are particularly relevant to you, or that are mentioned later in the book.

STRETCHING UPWARDS

Staying upright is the first thing to work on. One's instinct when asked to be upright is to try hard and tighten the muscles to achieve it, but this is not the effect we are after. A stiff rider is a cumbersome load.

When I ask a rider to stretch upwards I use images that help them to be upright without tensing up and losing that all important suppleness. The first image is to imagine yourself bouncing a ball on top of your head like a footballer, but not trying to head it into a goal, rather to keep it bouncing on top of your head. Or you can think of yourself as a puppet with a string attached to the top of your head, or as an African lady carrying a water jug on her head.

Most riders find one of those images useful as a way of stretching the back and the back of the neck upwards, of staying upright and poised without stiffening.

Another possibility is to go to the other extreme, so before stretching upwards, relax and sink down so that the body is as short as possible, then stretch up.

Riders who when off the horse slouch, round their shoulders and hunch over their desk at school or in the office, tend to ride with a rounded back. This does not look very elegant and you will find it difficult to move with the horse. The horse will tend to fall onto the forehand. So stretch upwards!

Riders who are rather tense, who make a big effort to sit up straight, usually tighten their muscles, hollow their back and may even lean back. This may look smarter than the rounded back, but the poor horse will find it uncomfortable to carry a stiff rider and will tighten the muscles in his back, making it hollow and forcing his head and neck upwards to come off the bit. So stretch upwards!

Stretching upwards might seem pretty simple, and maybe it is when you think about it. The problem is that when riding there are so many other things to think about, especially concerning the horse–controlling him, turning him, getting him going forward. All are important, but all will become easier if the rider is upright. Until you can stay upright consistently, make it a priority to think about it, and keep checking that you are actually doing it. With time, as long as you work at it, the muscles will develop that will make it easier to stay upright. Remember too it will become more natural to you and you will get the right muscles working properly sooner if you stay upright and stretching upwards even when you are off the horse.

> **Staying poised and upright needs persistence, determination, strengthening of the muscles and confidence.**

Sinking down and relaxing. This makes the stretch afterwards much more effective.

Stretching to be upright, and ideally without stiffening, is a most effective exercise for a rider.

STAYING UPRIGHT IN TURNS

This upward stretch is relatively easy to establish when standing still, a little harder when moving in a straight line, and for most riders pretty difficult in a turn. Some lean to one side as if they were turning a motorcycle, others drop their shoulder and collapse to the inside, others try to push the horse around, drop the outside shoulder and collapse to the outside. In all of these positions the poor horse is carrying an unbalanced load and it will be much harder for him to get around the turn. You need to focus on the upward stretch.

There is another thing to think about because the horse himself has turned. His shoulders and head are going in a different direction from when he was on a straight line. To stay in balance the rider has to turn with him. While keeping that upward stretch the rider has to turn his shoulders to keep them lined up with those of the horse, and without dropping his head, to keep his eyes focused on the ears so his head is turning with the horse's head. So many riders look to the inside in a turn and that puts an end to an upward stretch, throwing the rider out of balance with the horse.

Many riders find turning the shoulders awkward. What is worse is that one way is more difficult than the other. I find it useful to imagine you have two lights shining straight ahead from your chest (from your bosoms if you have any!) These lights need to be directed wherever you want the horse to go, so if you are turning right you have to turn your chest to the right.

To stay balanced in a turn, keep the body upright and turn the shoulders so that they are lined up with the horse's shoulders.

Check List

Keep stretching upwards.

Turn your shoulders with the horse's shoulders.

Focus your eyes on, or through, the ears.

Many riders think that taking the weight to the side means leaning in, but this produces the opposite effect, with the seat bones drifting to the outside of the saddle, along with the weight.

A good balanced position in a turn.

Looking through the ears and staying focused.

Lots of people are taught to look to the inside, but you lose the focus and the upright balanced position.

EXERCISES

Start on the ground, in front of a mirror, and get the hang of turning your shoulders and head to the left, then to the right, while keeping your spine and head upright, and your shoulders parallel to the ground (no dropping of one or the other). Progress to doing this on the horse when he is standing still, and then in the turns themselves.

CORRECTIONS

Few riders are naturally straight. Stretching up will help to iron out some kinks, but you will tend to drift back into long-held patterns. You will have to go back to stretching again and again. I have found that correcting weaknesses, like trying to lift a shoulder when one is dropped, is often counterproductive, not hitting the cause of the problem and setting up other tensions through trying so hard to make the correction.

For me there are two important points when making corrections. The first is to focus on the goal such as being poised, upright in the body or turning with the horse rather than making a correction like lifting a shoulder or taking one shoulder back. If you keep aiming for, thinking about and imagining the goal it tends to take you there. Secondly, if you do make a correction, remember that the problem is caused usually by tension in a block of muscles. So you need to let go of this tension rather than fighting it and setting up more tension. The best way to correct is to relax and let go as far as possible, then go into your stretch, turn or whatever.

The photograph right shows that riding with long stirrups helps to free the hips and allows the lower back to follow the movement of the horse, BUT only if the rider can keep the heels down and equal weight in both stirrups.

LENGTHENING DOWNWARDS

If asked what hits one about a good dressage rider's position most say long legs and very long stirrups. Some beginners try to copy this and put their stirrups down many holes, but usually end up groping for the stirrup; the toes go down and the rider is unstable in the saddle. Never ride so long that you cannot keep your heels down comfortably.

The reason for riding long is that it opens the angle of the hips, making it easier for the hip joint to move freely. Then the hips together with the other joints in the leg (knee and ankle) can act as better shock-absorbers. The problem is that you have to be pretty supple and relaxed for those muscles around the hip joint to do this. You need core stability (we are going to discuss that one later) in order to keep the muscles in the leg relaxed and avoid gripping with the knees. You have to progress by stages and it is no use aiming for these higher ones before the fundamentals are in place.

Start with stirrups that are the same length, and keep equal weight in them with the toes up and the whole leg resting against the horse and saddle, but not gripping.

There are two simple exercises (see exercise box) that help you achieve this and to gradually enable you to lengthen the stirrups without the toes tending to point downwards.

Exercise 1 helps to strengthen the leg muscles and to keep the heels down. It is a tough one and at first you may not be able to do it for very long but persist!

Taking the legs off the horse is one of the most effective exercises for establishing the best position for the legs. It releases any tendency to grip onto the saddle and stretches muscles that will help the legs to lengthen and let go.

Standing in the stirrups at the trot develops the leg muscles and stretches the area around the ankle joints—so helping to keep the heels down.

this at the trot and canter. If, however, you are riding a horse whose controls are not so good or whose back is so tight and stiff that it makes the sitting trot bumpy, it is best to keep to the walk.

It is proven that when you start riding a horse, whether he has been in the field or the stable you should spend 10 minutes or more in the walk to allow him to warm up and be ready for work. As long as it is safe to do so, cross your stirrups and ride without them during this first part of the training session. Allow your legs to drop as close to the ground as possible and use Exercise 2 again and again.

Exercise 2 is probably the most useful of all exercises for a dressage rider. You see international riders doing it, as it stretches the muscles around the hip joint, makes sure you are not gripping the saddle and puts your legs into an excellent position. I encourage riders to do it whenever they make the transition into walk, and as your seat becomes more secure you can do it in the trot or canter, although that is pretty difficult.

The other way of helping to lengthen the legs downward—to feel as if your heels are dropping down towards the earth—is to ride without stirrups. If you are lucky enough to have lunge lessons or to ride a schoolmaster then you can do

EXERCISES

1. In the trot find a position for yourself where you are in balance and do not have to sit in the saddle. Just keep out of the saddle for as long as you can manage. Let go of your knee and ankle joints and let your heels sink down towards the ground. When you first try it you can balance yourself with one or both hands.

2. Try this exercise first when the horse is standing still. Lift both legs off the horse, stretch them outwards and then let them drop downwards and backwards into place on the saddle and resting on the horse's sides.

Check List

Legs feel as if they are reaching for the ground, heels first.

Equal weight in both stirrups.

ALLOWING HANDS

Hands are British riders' number one handicap in their quest to be a Dressage Rider. We all want to use them as the main control—whether to stop, turn, or put the horse on the bit. The problem is that if used as the dominant aid the horse tries to avoid the nasty strong pressure in his mouth, tucks his head in or sticks it in the air and his hind legs go out behind. We are building up resistance and losing the power that comes from the hind quarters. For every inch that you pull back on the reins it stops the hind legs from coming forward by as much as 10 inches. This is not the way to work towards our goal of a Happy Athlete.

A free walk on a loose rein.

The effect of a rider holding the reins down, and with a backward tendency, is resistance—with the hind legs dropping out behind him.

We have to learn to ride with feeling hands that can receive messages from the mouth and allow the natural movement of the head and neck. Of course there are times when you have to give a check, occasionally a really big one, but then the important thing is to make it for one stride only (no hanging on), and if necessary give another one.

Although the aim is for a light contact between the hand and mouth, there may be times when it is pretty strong, particularly with the novice horse who may need support from the reins to balance or to learn to accept the contact.

Collecting the reins with allowing hands so that they follow the nod of the head rather than staying still and restricting it. The horse's steps do not slow down and barely shorten. The freedom is still there.

Only a small difference in approach from the rider but this time when collecting the reins the arms tighten, do not follow the nod of the head, and have a backward tendency. It makes a big difference on the horse who tightens his back, shortens his steps and is showing signs of a lateral walk with the hind and forelegs going in pairs.

It is still possible, however, for even a strong contact to be an allowing/forward feeling one, with the energy flowing forwards towards the bit. It is not necessary (and is destructive) to pull back or even fix your arms and hands for more than a stride or two; this applies a backward feeling pressure on the horse's mouth that will restrict his natural movement. Containing him with a backwards/restrictive feeling on the reins will spoil his natural ability.

To develop allowing, forward-feeling hands, start in the walk. You will see that the horse's head nods and the ears move. If you have allowing hands you will let them move and follow the nod. Your hands move back and forth and the rein contact will stay constant. If the hands stay still, the contact will have to change every stride and there will be a restrictive tension on the horse.

For the hands to be allowing, the arms and shoulders have to be relaxed. We often see tense riders with shoulders held up, closer to their ears than they need be. Aim to let the shoulder blades drop down, but do not forget the upward stretch of your spine, otherwise you may lose your uprightness. Dropping the blades should help the shoulders to be between the two extremes of being rounded or pulled back so far that they are tight. Of course they need to be level as well. The shoulder position is very important and often neglected.

When the shoulders are relaxed, the upper arms hanging down and not held in a position through tension, the arms and hands can move independently of the body and can keep a consistent contact by following and allowing the movement of the horse's head. When the arm muscles are relaxed, the elbows lie close to the rider's sides, not carried sticking out like wings. I often use the image that the elbows should feel that they have weights hanging from them. Then from the elbows the lower arms can become continuations of the reins. From the elbows to the bit are straight lines. The fingers should be closed on the reins, as if holding a sponge; the thumbs uppermost and resting on the rein.

I often tell riders to imagine they are holding a beer mug in each hand. That achieves the right position!

Check the effect of the other positions on your arms. If you turn your hands over with the backs of them uppermost, or if you hold them so high or low that there is a break in the line to the bit, you will feel the muscles in your arms tighten.

The hands, for most of the time, are held above the withers, and an equal distance from the bit. It is so common for one hand to drop

A positive but light elastic contact.

lower than the other and/or for one to be closer to the bit than the other; correcting this is surprisingly difficult. Riders cannot believe that they are riding with unequal heights or lengths and I usually ask them to put knots in their reins at the same distance from the bit and to keep their hands close to these.

> It is really, really important to work on establishing allowing hands that fall into a good position—so persist!

EXERCISES

A good exercise for loosening the shoulders. Firstly lift them close to your ears and then let them fall down.

- Whenever you start riding in the walk period make sure you have allowing hands by following the nodding of the horse's head. After some minutes in a free walk on a long rein, gather the reins without him shortening his steps or slowing down. You can only do this if your hands are allowing and you support with your legs.

- Lift your shoulders as close to your ears as you can get them and then let them drop down—this is a good way of relieving the tension and can be done at any time when you are riding.

- If you pull back, bridge your reins like jockeys do when racing.

- If you move your hands a lot, or hold them unevenly, carry a short stick under both thumbs and at right angles to the reins

- To get your shoulders in a good position, pull your breast bone back towards the shoulder blades (see picture on page 22)

Check List

Relax your shoulders and let them drop downwards.

Keep the elbows resting close to the body.

Carry the hands with thumbs uppermost and both the same height and distance from the bit.

Relax the arms enough to be able to follow the movement of the horse's head.

Whether taking a strong, light or no contact, feel that your hands are directed/pointing towards the bit.

THE AIDS

When you are stretching the back, with the back of the neck and head up, the legs lengthening down, and the hands allowing, your aids are going to become much more effective. Your horse is going to have a lighter and more stable burden to carry and he will be able to distinguish your aids more clearly.

You will have been using aids since you first started riding: usually a pullback to stop, a pull on the inside rein to turn, and a kick to go forward. It is, however, very important to know just what you can do with your hands, legs, and seat, so that you can gradually learn to co-ordinate the way in which you use them to communicate better with your horse and make them an instinctive part of your riding.

WAYS THE HANDS CAN BE USED

ALLOWING HANDS

We have already looked at this: how to develop the allowing feeling—allowing a forward feeling while keeping a consistent elastic contact with the mouth. This is the way in which we use the hands most of the time, in a supportive way, always in communication with the mouth but neither allowing so much that you lose the contact nor have such a dead contact that the horse can lean on it.

Open fingers as in the photograph on left, do not establish a consistent elastic contact with the mouth. Keep them closed.

The photograph below shows the fingers closed but relaxed, helping the arms and shoulders to stay relaxed, able to follow the movement and to keep consistent contact.

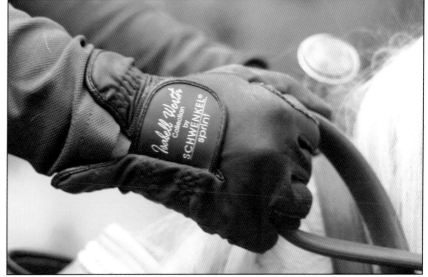

Fingers clenched; arm and shoulder muscles will tighten, too, and provide the non-allowing rein aid.

A light check when one hand is lifted and taken back a little, but for no longer than during one stride.

NON-ALLOWING HANDS

This is when you stop allowing by clenching your fingers on the reins and tightening the muscles in the arms so that they cannot be pulled forward. This way you block the forward momentum and can achieve movements such as going from trot to walk or coming to a standstill.

THE CHECK

Very occasionally with a trained horse, but more frequently when jumping, going across country or with a horse that has been given little schooling, the non-allowing hand does not work. Then you have to give a check, a strong pull on the rein upward and or backwards BUT the really important thing is that it is short and the pressure is released after no more than one stride. You may have to apply a check again to get the result you want, but not for longer than one stride.

SOFTENING

This is when messages are sent down the rein by moving the fingers like a piano player or by turning the wrist inwards so the thumb is pointing towards the other hand and then back

Softening can be achieved by moving the fingers or turning the wrist inwards, with the thumb pointing towards the other hand, as in this picture.

A yielding of the contact is used as a reward and after a half-halt.

to the normal position. These actions that have a softening effect on the jaw or poll are a way of asking for flexion at the poll and of preparing the horse for a turn. They will only have a softening effect if there is no pull back. Use only variations both to the pressure and where it falls in the horse's mouth. Many riders try to pull the neck around or see saw the head and neck from side to side to make the horse soften. Be warned—although the horse might be shocked into rounding up at first, it is painful and restrictive for him and he will usually start to resist more. This is not the way to turn him into a happy athlete!

YIELDING

The hands go forward to lighten or even give up the contact for a stride. This is used by riders to check that they are not using too strong a contact, or as a reward to the horse, thanking him for doing something well. Yielding without losing the contact for a longer time allows the horse to stretch forward and down—a very important exercise that we shall come to later.

WAYS THE LEGS CAN BE USED

FORWARD-DRIVING

This is when both legs are used by or just behind the girth to encourage the horse to go forward and to build up his energy. Ideally he should respond to light nudges, but occasionally a stronger kick may be necessary.

SUPPORTIVE

The leg or legs rest on the horse's side in a supportive role. When one is placed a little further back it guards the quarters from drifting out to that side. There is a positive contact but not an active one—no kicking.

FORWARD SIDEWAYS

One leg is used actively to encourage the horse to step forwards and sideways as in the lateral movements.

The forward-driving leg aid that is applied close to the girth.

The forward-sideways leg aid that is applied further back.

WAYS THE WEIGHT CAN BE USED

The more you advance in dressage the more you depend on the weight aids, but before this is possible you do need a balanced and secure position. I will cover them in more detail later in the book.

WEIGHT TO ONE SIDE

Putting more weight on one side, down the leg and into the stirrup (and as you advance on the seat bone). This will help to turn the horse to that side. It is a really effective aid BUT only if the rider keeps the stretch upwards, lengthens the legs and has allowing hands. It is very easy to try to get the weight over by leaning or collapsing which loses any benefit.

WEIGHT ON THE SEAT BONES

The direction and the amount of weight put onto the seat bones will have a big effect on the way that a trained dressage horse goes. It can be used to produce a collecting effect, a forward driving effect, and helps the horse to move through the back but not until the horse is pretty well trained and the rider has a good degree of core stability.

In the photograph on the right the rider is putting more weight into the inside stirrup while staying upright in the body. This is helping the horse to turn right off the track.

CHAPTER 2
FOLLOWING THE MOVEMENT

By now, stretching, lengthening and allowing should be almost second nature to you, so that you feel pretty stable and secure on your horse and you also look good. The next stage is to follow the movement of the horse, to use that rather odd term, 'swing with the hips'.

An athletic horse will use all his muscles, his body will be free and supple, which means that his back muscles will be constantly relaxing and contracting (known as a 'swinging back'). The rider has to follow this movement if he is not to disturb and restrict it. He has to be able to 'swing with the hips'—small fluent movements of a supple but passive lower back.

CORE STABILITY

To follow the movement it is important to develop core stability, a concept that not just riders but all athletes work on nowadays. It means that you have a firm balanced base (your pelvis) enabling everything else in the body to work more freely.

Jenny Iles, a Pilates instructor, demonstrates:

(Opposite). The upright pelvis. A useful indicator of this key position is a pole that will touch the back of the head, shoulder-blades and bottom.

(Above, left). Leaning back, the pelvis tipping backwards.

(Above, right). The hollow back with the pelvis tipping forwards.

Your deep postural muscles support your upright posture, and your arms and legs can move independently. For any ambitious rider this needs serious study.

A BALANCED BASE

The rider's base is the pelvis and this has to be upright if the other parts stemming from it—downwards the thigh bones (from the hip sockets) and upwards the spine—can be in their most balanced positions and able to move freely.

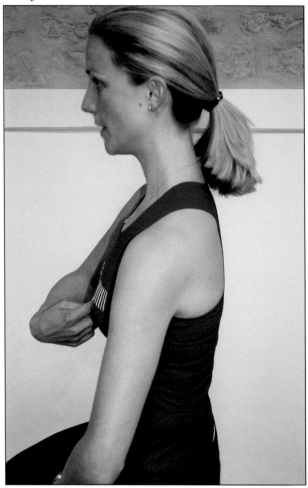

The shoulder blades are flat. To help achieve this, gently push back the breast bone as the Pilates teacher, Jenny Iles, is doing.

The seat bones are the lowest points of the pelvis and they are the ones that you should feel resting securely in the saddle. The harder part is to make sure that:

- They are carrying equal weight (otherwise the pelvis is higher one side than the other) and
- They are level, one is not further forward than the other (otherwise the pelvis is twisted).

By feeling where the seat bones are, the rider can decide whether the pelvis is level and straight: i.e. not twisted or higher on one side than the other.

How do you know when the pelvis is upright?

Stretching upwards started the process, and again the seat bones can be used as indicators. When the pelvis tips forward you roll onto a more forward part of the bones and press down

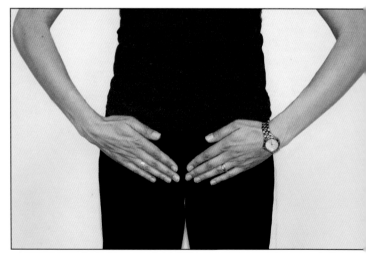

The triangle formed by these hands indicates the key muscles needed for core stability: the transversus abdominis. This is the area to strengthen in order to develop core stability.

on the crotch, and if it tips backward you come off the tips and onto the back part of your bottom. The aim is the classical three-point seat. If the pubic bone and the two seat bones can be felt in the saddle, the pelvis is close to upright.

TIPPING FORWARD AND BACK

Going to the extremes deliberately is another way of establishing the feel for the position. Tip your pelvis forward by hollowing your back and pushing your waist forward. Then tip it back by leaning back or by holding in the top of your tummy and rounding your back. What you want is to be in the middle of these two extremes.

SECURITY IN THE UPRIGHT POSITION

To be able to hold the pelvis securely upright needs strong postural muscles and a stomach that is not flabby but held so that it is relatively flat and firm. For the technical it is the *transversus abdominis* muscles that play the key role. They form a triangle running from the pubic bone at the front up to two points a couple of inches below the waist (see photo p.22). They are the only abdominal muscles that run from the front through to the lumbar vertebrae at the rear and as such can, if used, give support to the lower back.

The upright pelvis is the stable core around which the rest of your body can move freely, your spine can stretch upwards, your legs and arms can move independently and your hips can swing. It is the basis of poise and that is a feature of a really good dressage position on the horse.

If you have a chance to take Pilates classes, this will help you to develop your core stability.

Check List

Pelvis upright.

Seat bones carrying equal weight.

Seat bones level.

EXERCISES

Images are always a good way of learning a technique holistically. Imagine standing on the edge of a cliff and peering over it. To stop yourself falling over you will stretch upwards and bring into action your postural stomach muscles. You can do this when riding your horse.

Using a Fitness Ball, push the top of your pelvis forwards, then backwards, then let it rest in the middle in the upright position. Breathe in through your nose and feel the breath going into your back and expanding the ribcage laterally. Then breathe out forcefully through pursed lips, tightening your front tummy muscles (without tipping your pelvis) and bringing your ribcage down. Hold this position while taking a number of breaths, then release and repeat. Take care that your shoulders do not tighten and that you are letting the shoulder blades drop down. Some hold this position on a Fitness Ball when watching TV or working at a desk. That helps to develop the postural muscles—it is good for your riding and for healthy use of your body.

The key muscle in achieving a flattened, resilient stomach is the *transversus abdominis* and it helps to activate it when you make your out-breaths forceful and if you pull up your pelvic floor. The Pilates teacher Jenny Iles says you can imagine the deep pelvic floor contracting, like an elevator moving up to the top floor!

SUPPLENESS

The greater your core stability, and your balance, the easier it will be for you to develop that other key element in a dressage rider—suppleness. It is no use trying to be very supple until stretching, lengthening, allowing and being stable in the saddle have become second nature because then you just flop, and most likely into the wrong position. There is no avoiding some tension and stiffness in the early stages of becoming a dressage rider. To develop the correct frame for a rider—to be upright—may seem strange and take considerable effort to achieve. Initially there is likely to be tension. Do not worry about it, but as and when you feel more confident about keeping upright, start to work on your suppleness.

As with your horse, you are aiming for no resistance in the muscles so that they can do their job of contracting and relaxing. The joints need to be able to move freely, not fixed in a position by tight muscles.

Beware of trying too hard, as this tightens the muscles. Exercises that will help the muscles, ligaments and joints to work freely and so develop suppleness are the stretching and strengthening ones, and again Pilates is recommended. Taking some deep breaths is a good way of releasing tension, and therefore promoting suppleness.

When a rider has developed a rounded position (as demonstrated above), he needs to get upright. For a while this may mean stiffening,, as seen in the picture below. The suppleness can be worked on after the uprightness has been established.

MENTAL TOUGHNESS

Suppleness depends on your mental as well as your physical state. If you are nervous or tense this will affect your body and will stop it working freely. You need to be focused, but relaxed and confident, on the horse. Confidence will be reflected in your position: you will tend to be more upright, more poised and more supple when you achieve it. The young dressage star Laura Bechtolsheimer said that her straight, strong position came with her growing confidence. With confidence, she did not collapse or tense up when things started to go wrong, and could handle problems.

Confidence and relaxation are an important part of suppleness. If you do suffer from nerves, there are many excellent books or courses on mental training that will help not just your riding but also your approach towards exams and any other tests.

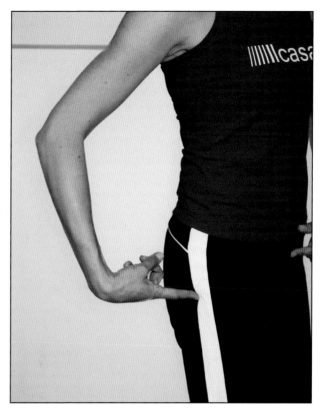

The hip socket cannot be felt, so many have no idea where it is! Jenny Iles is pointing to where it lies behind layers of body tissue.

Check List

Develop awareness of where you are tense.

Let go of tensions

Work towards being focused and relaxed.

SWINGING HIPS: WHAT DOES IT MEAN?

The first thing is to know where the thigh bone connects with the pelvis at the hip socket. This is hard to feel, but it is in the crease between the leg and the stomach. This socket is well protected – so well protected that it is usually rather fixed. It helps if the muscles around it are able to contract and relax freely, opening the angle of the hip joint so that the leg hangs down pretty straight makes this easier. At the same time the pelvis needs to be upright so it is not fixed in a forward or backward position. The spine needs to be stretched upwards so that the load is light – not like a sack of potatoes – and the mobile vertebrae (those in the lower back) are free to move.

The result of all this freeing-up is to enable you to follow the movement of the horse who, if working correctly, will have a supple swinging back (more about that later).

We recognize a rider who swings with the hips, because the movement of the horse is taken by the lower back. There is no head – nodding, tipping of the upper body back and forward, or legs wobbling around. In the trot there is no 'bumping trot' with the rider sitting rigidly and just going up and down. Instead the rider swings softly and almost imperceptibly with the movement.

The important thing when learning to 'swing with the hips' is for the rider to allow his lower back to move, but not to direct it. The movement in the lower back happens because the rider is secure, upright and supple in the saddle and is so connected to the horse's movement that he or she can passively and fluently follow this movement.

Another help in the learning process is to ride a horse that has a supple swinging back to teach you the feel. So many older horses and those who have not had correct training have stiff backs, and riding them feels like holding a road drill: lots of shuddering, and an uncomfortable up and down movement! To make your horse a happy athlete you want all the muscles to work, particularly over the back, and then he will have that soft swinging movement that is easy to sit to.

If you do not learn to 'swing with your hips' you will teach your horse to become one of these shuddering movers, so it is well worth coming to terms with this rather obscure concept.

It takes courage to be able to let go of the muscles in the lower back; to allow the hips to swing and follow the movement of the horse. Be brave and then you will be able to come into a better harmony with a happier athlete.

Check List

An upright pelvis gives the lower back the greatest potential to swing.

Allow the lower back to take the movement.

Stretch upwards and free up the joints.

Stay passive, just focus on the movement in the horse's back rather than directing your own.

Although it is vital to swing with the hips, remember that it is a barely perceptible movement, hardly visible to the onlooker.

EXERCISES

Learn to take the movement by not letting yourself be moved out of the saddle and holding onto the front of the saddle or a strap. Do not let your lower back tighten and stiffen. If it does, go into rising trot, or forward seat in the canter, or back to the walk, until you can loosen up and allow the lower back to become supple again.

With an upright pelvis this rider is able to follow the movement of the walk, allowing the horse to move through the back.

FOLLOWING THE MOVEMENT IN WALK

The walk is by far the easiest pace to sit to, as there is no moment of suspension to throw the rider around. It is, however, vital that the horse does not tighten and stiffen his back muscles, otherwise he will shorten his steps and/or lose the correct rhythm for the pace (four-time marching pace) and turn into a pacer (two-time walk). In a dressage test this loses you many marks as the most important criterion for good dressage training is to maintain and enhance the horse's natural ability which includes the correctness of the paces. See page 53.

Any disturbance to the correct rhythm of a pace, whether it is the walk, trot or canter, is a very serious fault, and the easiest one to disturb is the walk.

You want to keep the horse's back supple, and to do this you have to allow the muscles to contract and relax freely. The rider's lower back needs to follow the movement, and if it does he will find that first one seat bone then the other swings forward. The horse's hind leg lifts the rider's seat bone on the same side and takes it forward as he steps forward. It is a similar motion to the way we walk and I had a wonderful moment when teaching a disabled rider who is normally confined to a wheelchair. Once she was on the horse, I asked her to let go in the lower back and follow the horse's movement with her seat bones. Suddenly there were shouts of joy: "I am walking. I am walking", as one seat bone then the other was taken forward.

FOLLOWING THE MOVEMENT IN TROT

This is much more difficult to follow than the walk, because in the trot the horse moves his legs in diagonal pairs, and as each pair swings back it pushes the horse into the air for a short moment of suspension when the horse has no feet on the ground. There is bounce to the movement, and unless the rider wants the horse to lose the natural expression and move along with short stiff strides that never leave the ground, he has to be able to follow this movement with the lower back.

THE RISING TROT

There is an easy way of achieving the movement and that is with the rising trot. To avoid the bump, the rider rises when one diagonal pair of fore and hind legs comes off the ground, and sits when it returns to the ground. If the rider always rose with the same diagonal, the horse would become one-sided, so remember to change diagonals. The convention is to rise on the inside diagonal. When working on the left rein, rise as the inside left hind comes off the ground, and on the right rein for the inside right hind.

To be a dressage rider you need to focus on the hind legs and to feel what they are doing. However, as long as you do not tip forward too much, you can check which diagonal you are on by looking at the movement of the shoulder. So on the left rein you should rise as the right shoulder swings forward. Note: in the photograph, the rider is riding on the outside diagonal.

In rising trot you have to find a balance so that there is no jerkiness to your movement. The upper body can tip forward slightly, but too much and the horse will tend to fall onto the forehand, too little and your movement will not be fluent.

Another aid to fluency is to avoid rising very high. Allow the horse to push you out of the saddle as the inside hind swings forward.

A good exercise to help the ankle joints relax is to let your heels sink down nearer the ground every time you rise out of the saddle. This is only possible if your legs do not ride up and if you are not gripping with your knees. If your legs are lifting up and your toes tipping down, use more often the exercise of taking your legs off the horse whenever you return to walk; and stay out of the saddle when in trot (see page 10).

Rising to the trot in a good balance.

There is this idea that dressage riders have to do sitting trot, but it is not correct. The Number One Aim is to have the horse working in a good way and if the trot strides become flat or tight always go back to rising trot. I have seen Grand Prix riders doing their passage and half-passes in rising trot: so rise to the trot whenever you feel that the horse's movement is becoming restricted.

Check List

Keep your movement fluent.

Find the line, just in front of the vertical where you are balanced.

Let your heels sink down every time you rise.

Change diagonals.

THE SITTING TROT

When learning to take the movement in the sitting trot, you might have to put your horse through some times when you are a stiff burden for him to carry. It is great to learn on an older schoolmaster who knows the form and one who does not have big movement that is difficult to sit to.

When starting to learn to sit to the trot, only ask your horse for slow, short strides, so that it is easier to follow the movement. The important thing is that you follow the movement, do not tighten, and just go up and down. If you feel you are tightening and losing your security, return to walk or rising trot.

Be brave: allow your hips to swing and let your lower back move with the horse, but remember – no directing of the movement, no pumping as we sometimes see. Nor should there be any tendency to collapse the back, which has to stay stretched so that the weight is light and the lower back is not squashed into the saddle.

Check List

Stretch upwards.

Let go in your lower back.

Be confident and courageous rather than nervous and tense.

EXERCISES

One of the best ways of learning how to ride the sitting trot well is simply to watch good riders, and imagine that you are riding. Dressage techniques are catching. Watching and working with riders who have good positions will help you to achieve one for yourself.

Put a strap across the front of your saddle and as soon as, or before, you feel your seat bones coming out of the saddle and your muscles tensing, catch hold of it.

Work on the lunge, with a safe horse and a good trainer

Work without stirrups, but only after you have warmed up your horse, and when his back is supple.

Sitting to the trot with a good upright back. Perfection is difficult and ideally the legs could have been further back!

Again, in the canter this rider is able to stay upright, allowing the lower back to take the movement.

FOLLOWING THE MOVEMENT IN CANTER

Whilst the trot is the bouncy movement, the canter is the springing one, or at least it should be. You see some riders feeling rather happy that they can sit tall and control the horse in what I call the 'comfy canter'. The problem is that the strides are flat, the beat is not what it is by nature and the muscles are not working freely. The horse is not working in the athletic way that we seek in dressage.

FORWARD SEAT

To help the horse move his back freely and spring into a moment of suspension, you can lighten the weight in the saddle. The forward seat used for going across country and jumping is also useful in dressage. It is a good way for the rider to find a balance in the canter; it helps the horse to move athletically; and it is a useful

These photographs show just how much movement there can be in the canter from the downhill to the uphill steps in each and every stride.

method of warming up the horse and encouraging him to work more freely. It is difficult to stay balanced in the forward seat if your stirrups are long, so if you feel uncomfortable, shorten them.

By nature the horse springs into the air at each canter stride, there is a clear three-beat and a defined leading leg so the movement on one side is different from the other. One side of the horse is slightly ahead of the other so to follow the movement the rider has one seat bone slightly more forward than the other.

As in the walk and trot, the rider has to allow the lower back to follow the movement. In the canter this is an uphill feeling as the outside hind returns to the ground then a downhill one as the horse tips forward until just the leading foreleg is on the ground before it lifts off into the moment of suspension. It all happens very quickly and the rider can focus on little more than staying upright and allowing the lower back to follow the movement. So many riders tighten their muscles and then we see their body rocking back and forth. Other riders find it difficult to keep the muscles around the hip joints free; they grip with the knees, their legs ride up and the toes drop down.

As with the trot be brave and let the lower back follow the movement.

Check list

Stretch upwards.

Allow the lower back to follow the movement that is like a very small jump every stride.

EXERCISES
FOR THE CANTER

Ride in the forward seat to get your balance. Hold onto a strap/piece of string that is attached to the D's at the front of the saddle to help keep your balance and your seat bones in the saddle.

Whenever you stop cantering and go into the walk, take your legs off the horse to release the tightening of the legs and the gripping with the knees. As your balance improves, a less exaggerated version of this exercise can be done in the canter.

Lean back behind the vertical in the canter for a circuit, as this helps to stretch some of the muscles that need to work freely for you to follow the movement.

Following the movement in a transition from the diagonal two-time trot (opposite above) into the four-time marching walk (opposite below).

FOLLOWING THE MOVEMENT IN TRANSITIONS

This is often neglected and is quite difficult as, for example, from trot to walk you have to allow the lower back to change from following a two-time rhythm to a four-time one. From canter to trot there is a change from a three-time asymmetrical movement to a two-time symmetrical one. You need to be aware that this is what is going to happen, and to allow your lower back to make the adjustments. Then practise!

Often in the all-important trot/walk transition you see the rider changing from rising to sitting trot, and a sitting trot in which the rider's back is tight and stifling the movement and then having to pull on the reins to get a reaction to go into the walk. There is no problem in remaining in rising trot; you can still use your weight as an aid for the transition and you are not stifling the movement.

The essential factor, as always, is to allow the horse to keep moving freely and not to stifle the freedom of the muscles. When the muscles (particularly those in the back) tighten, the horse's steps will tend to get shorter and stiffer and that will affect the rhythm and fluency of the transitions.

CHAPTER 3

INFLUENCING THE MOVEMENT

The rider can influence the movement by making the horse's steps:

- more expressive and elastic,
- shorter and higher (the collecting effect),
- longer (the extending effect),
- faster and slower (changing the tempo),
- more balanced (taking the weight back and engaging the quarters),
- straighter (more upright and hindlegs stepping towards the forelegs).

All of these effects will be looked at in the following pages when we focus on the training of the horse. Here, in this section, the training of the rider, we need to consider the most important tools in achieving these effects – the use of the back and the half-halt.

USING THE BACK

The rider who is balanced, upright and following the movement of the horse in walk, trot (sitting), canter and transitions is ready to bring in the use of the back as an additional aid.

The back is used when applying what are called the 'weight' or 'seat' aids. How it is used

This figure shows the use of the back when collecting. The dotted lines indicate the key muscles involved.

This figure shows the use of the back when extending, and again the dotted lines indicate the key muscles involved.

DRIVING EFFECT

Secondly there is the back that encourages the horse to work more forwards and extend the steps. Tighten the buttock and stomach muscles and slightly round the back to encourage the forward thrust of the hind legs.

LIGHTENING EFFECT

Thirdly the weight on the seat bones can be lightened, by putting more onto the thighs and stirrups but without leaning forwards. This can help the horse's back to soften and move more freely, and is also a reward for the horse – like the yielding rein aid.

DIRECTIONAL EFFECT

Fourthly more weight can be transferred onto one seat bone than the other. This use of the weight encourages the horse to move, turn or bend in that direction. While keeping the body upright the rider lightens one seat bone and puts more weight on the other and down through the leg into the stirrup.

may differ from person to person according to the way they are made and how they are taught. Also it is not that easy for anybody, not even experts, to understand exactly what is happening in the back as there is a mass of muscles, bones, ligaments and nerves all playing their part. I am just going to describe the essence— what it feels like.

COLLECTING EFFECT

Firstly there is the back that helps to collect the steps. Tighten the muscles in the buttocks and all the way up the back of the back. You feel as if you have grown a little taller and are asking the horse to lift his shoulders and be contained into moving with shorter and higher strides.

Check List

Keep stretching upwards with the back and lengthening downwards with the legs.

The back can be used for collecting, extending, and encouraging freer movement.

The weight can be used to turn and to move laterally.

The back is used together with other aids.

Momentary use, that can be repeated, is more effective than when fixed for a longer time.

THE HALF-HALT

For the novice rider and horse the half-halt is no more than a check on one or both reins. The key factor is that the check should last no longer than one stride. If necessary, reapply it until the

The half-halt showing the rider 'enclosing' the horse with the leg, seat and hand aids.

horse responds. When only the rein aids are used, however, the horse will tend to hollow and lose engagement. For the rider who has learnt to follow the movement of the horse, there are immense new possibilities through use of a more subtle half-halt.

THE AIM

The check form of the half-halt was a clear message to the horse to slow down, shorten the steps and stop leaning onto the forehand. The real half-halt is much more. The aim is for the hind legs to step a little further under, and for the stride to shorten and to heighten slightly, so that the horse becomes a little rounder without any loss of suppleness and softness.

The rider asks the horse to go forward but blocks him from doing so with non-allowing hands. The forward thrust from the hind legs goes through the back and neck and rebounds back from the bit and encourages the hind legs to be more active and engage. The horse is 'enclosed' momentarily by the rider between the legs, seat, and hands.

It is very much individual to each rider exactly how this is achieved, and different approaches can influence the movement in different ways. Whatever the variations, it is necessary to keep the goals, and images clearly in the mind.

POSSIBLE AIDS

A pretty effective approach is momentarily, for no more than one stride, to use the collecting effect of the back (see previous page) and stop following the movement of the horse. At the same time close the legs on the horse and stop allowing with the hands (clench the fingers and tighten the arms). The horse is closed up like a coiled spring that is pushed and held together. Then these three aids are released, and momentarily the reins are yielded slightly.

DEVELOPING THE HALF-HALT

When in the trot, giving the aids for a transition to walk, but releasing the aids before he has time to make the transition, is a useful way of developing the feel for a half-halt.

MOMENTARY AIDS

All of this takes place in an instant; if the aids are held in place any longer, the horse starts to resist and to lose that crucial suppleness. However, although the half-halt lasts for a very, very short time, it can be used again and again. Repetitive actions are much more effective than one long one. The aim is for a single half-halt to have barely visible results, but for a series of them to produce profound results.

SLOW PROGRESS

To do a good half-halt needs a well-trained horse and a very good rider, but not so good half-halts still have many benefits and help the rider to keep improving their skills. So be satisfied with very little; only ask for as much as the horse will accept without tightening; keep your aids light. Over time, as long as your half-halts are not producing resistance, they will help you to be a good dressage rider.

Check List

Apply the aids simultaneously.

Apply the aids for no more than one stride.

Finish with a slight yield of the reins.

Only ask as much as your horse will give without resistance.

Do not give up. Progress may be slow but nonetheless can be very influential.

EXERCISES

Use the trot/walk/trot transition to get a feel for the action of a half-halt and turn it into a half-halt by applying the aids for walk then releasing them immediately—before the horse walks.

So many riders stop doing half-halts because either they feel they are not making much difference or that the horse is tensing against the aids. Keep asking for very little. One or two or even twenty or thirty of these tiny half-halts may not make an impression, but thousands, over the course of months will—so don't give up!

FEEL

This is the icing on the cake for any rider, and is a big aid in turning the rider into someone who influences rather than passively follows the movement.

Good riders ooze feel—so what is it?

Feel does not come so much from knowledge of how to do it but from experience and from the natural ability to listen to the horse and to know how to react. A natural empathy with the horse is also very important; so is plenty of experience of how horses move, react, and think. To be effective, feel needs to become instinctive. Instant reactions are key to putting it to good use.

Although we usually think of feel as a natural talent it can be developed both through experience and having the confidence and relaxation to listen to the horse.

With feel a rider:

- Realises what a horse is about to do and can react accordingly to stop or to help it happen. For example, the rider may feel that the horse is about to (a) fall from canter into trot so drives him more forward; or (b) to gallop off, so calms him and takes firm control.

- Knows when a horse is tired and needs a rest, or lazy and needs firm aids.

- Can find the speed in which the horse works best, neither so fast that he becomes tense or so slow that he is lazy.

- Uses the aids at the right moment and as hard or as softly as the horse needs to obey.

- Realizes when the horse is about to resist and can decide quickly whether to make the exercise easier, or to ask less of him, or to give stronger aids.

- Is aware of faults in their early stages and can then correct them when it is easier to do so.

- Reacts immediately when a horse yields by lightening the aids.

Check List

Listen to the horse.

Be confident and relaxed as tight muscles stop the feel getting through to you.

Get as much experience as possible of riding different horses.

CHAPTER 4
OBEDIENCE
AND TRUST

When riding a horse, obedience has to be the first goal for without it you are going to have a pretty dangerous time. The second goal, trust, is almost as important, as then there is no danger of obedience being forced out of the horse; it is achieved through a logical system that the horse can understand. This means that you have to make very clear what you want—good use of the aids. Then through repetition, use of rewards (pats, voice, yielding of the reins and sugar) when he does it right; and reprimands (growls, taps with the whip, stronger aids, repeated demands) when he does it wrong. In this way we make good use of the horse's fantastic memory and he learns that he will be happier if he obeys the rider.

The reward—a release of the inside rein and a friendly pat/rub close to the wither. This small movement will not disturb the balance like a big pat.

Check List

Use clear consistent aids.

Apply for a short time only, and repeat until obedience is achieved.

Use a system of reward and reprimand to make use of the horse's great memory and to teach him to obey.

STOPPING

It is pretty frightening to go forward unless you know you can stop! You want your horse to do this willingly and with minimum use of reins—otherwise you are likely to forfeit trust. He will start to resist against painful pulling in his mouth so you want to teach him to stop without doing this.

The first thing he can learn is that some term like 'whoaa' means to slow down or stop. With a young horse it is a good idea to do this on the lunge and when leading him. Then when you ride him, always say 'whoaa' at the same time as you apply the rein aid—the check for one stride only. Using these two aids together will help to minimise the strength and the number of times you have to repeat the rein aid before he obeys. If he is not listening to the aids, use your voice and checks when heading towards a high wall or boards. He will have to stop, and then you can give him his reward. Try again and, if successful, start to ask him to stop or slow down when there is no wall in front of him.

Applying a check . . .

. . . and stopping in a halt.

As long as you use clear aids and a reward when he obeys, he is likely to understand, to trust you and to obey pretty quickly.

In the following pages we shall discuss how the legs and seat are brought into the equation so that the way the horse slows down or stops is more athletic. But the first step is just to make him obedient and reacting to light, simple aids.

Check List

Start if possible on the lunge or leading in hand.

Use checks on the rein and the voice.

Reward as soon as he slows down or stops.

GOING FORWARD

The most common solution that skilled trainers use when the horse is being difficult is to make him go forward. Because the horse is such a powerful animal we do tend to hold him back and we need to be courageous and ask him to work more freely forward (as long as we can stop!).

Going forward very willingly.

BEND AND FLEXION

We have talked about bend and flexion in the turning of the horse, and it is important to know what they both mean. They are not the same thing.

In flexion the horse turns his head around the joint where his head and neck join. When you ask for flexion, soften a little with the rein on one side. The neck stays straight and the head turns so that you can see his eye and nostril—just. It is a very small turn, but a very important one, as it is only when this area is soft and mobile that the horse will feel good in your hands. Also it is flexion that is always asked for first, before any bend.

Many riders pull back on the rein to try and get a flexion. Even if it is only a slight backward tendency the horse's usual reaction to this is to tighten his muscles against the pull and/or shorten his neck in an effort to avoid it.

To bend, the horse's body is bent uniformly around the rider's inside leg; it will follow the line of the turn or circle so that the hind legs step forward into the same tracks as the forelegs. If the bend is merely a bend in the neck from the withers, this will make it difficult for him to keep balanced, and the forward thrust from the hind legs will be lost out of the outside shoulder as mentioned above.

This is all that is needed for flexion. The rider can see the eye, but there is no bend in the neck.

Remember that a horse has to be quite supple if he is to show an obvious bend in this correct way around the rider's leg. It takes much training to achieve this, so in the beginning be satisfied with very little. He might feel almost straight, but all that is needed is a flexion at the poll. and a slight bend to be in the direction of the turn, not to the outside.

Check List

Flexion is a slight turn of the horse's head only.

Bend is uniform along the horse's body and is centred around the rider's inside leg.

Be satisfied with very little flexion and bend, as long as they are correct.

EXERCISES

Ride down a straight line, if possible towards a mirror. Keep the horse's neck and body straight; ask for a slight flexion to one side; then straighten him for a few strides and flex him to the other side without slowing down, speeding up or creating any resistance. This gives you a feel for flexion, but it is not easy, so do not ask for very much.

Use the figure-of-eight, serpentines and circles to develop the ability to flex, bend and turn.

The difference when the head is straight. Note that the rein is now touching the neck.

See also section on Turns (page 66)

CHAPTER 5
THE FUNDAMENTALS FOR THE HORSE

Our goal is to make the horse a happy athlete. British riders are famous for their horsemanship, and are very good at teaching obedience and earning trust. These form a crucial basis, but there is much more we need to develop if the horse is to be a real athlete who works in harmony with the rider.

Dressage has a long history. It was practised as far back as Classical Greek times; on the Parthenon frieze, horses are depicted performing all sorts of dressage movements. Over the centuries, methods of training have become more and more effective and humane. Riders from many different countries have played a part in this development, but it was the Germans who, at the beginning of the last century, collected the ideas together and established the Scales of Training—the basics—just like scales for the piano.

These Training Scales have been tested over the last hundred years and found to be a wonderful guide. They have helped Germany to become the

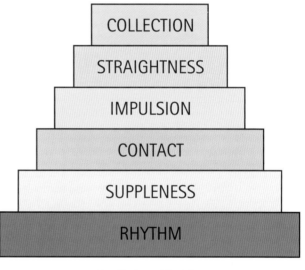

The Scales of Training

leading dressage nation winning every single team gold medal for thirty successive years. Riders have based their training on the Scales, whether for a young horse or a Grand Prix horse. Today they are recognised by the ruling international equestrian organisation (Fédération Equestre Internationale) and have been adopted as the basis of all judging.

If you really want to turn your horse into a happy athlete I can only advise you to learn the six scales inside out and develop clear images of them. They are the most important goals for your horse, and you need to refer back to them constantly, especially if you hit a problem. Other people have tried other ways but none have stood the test of time so well, and today the training scales are attracting ever-increasing numbers of recruits.

HOW TO USE THE SCALES OF TRAINING

First of all learn them by heart like your alphabet. They are Rhythm, Suppleness, Contact, Impulsion, Straightness and Collection.

Then build up really clear images of what they really mean. Twenty years on from first starting to work with the Training Scales, every time I listen to lectures, watch demos, read in books about them, or at times when I am working on them in training I find another dimension to them. So even if you can recite the definitions keep yourself open to learning more about them. When you are riding you need to be constantly asking yourself:

Has he got rhythm?
Is he supple?
How is the contact, etc?

When you first start working towards these goals you may not find much rhythm, but you may be pleased when he softens just a tiny bit. Be satisfied with small improvements and do not expect your horse to show the same degree of suppleness as a Grand Prix or even an Elementary horse. That does not make it any less important, however, for you to work on the suppleness.

The Training Scales are the goals you are working towards whenever you do an exercise or a movement, whether it is a free-rein walk, a circle, transition, shoulder-in or piaffe. They are the goals for the exercise, and if you keep the rhythm, suppleness etc, through the exercise it will help you to improve the Scales, as well as being the key elements in doing an exercise well. Therefore I am not going to list exercises that will help develop the Scales. According to what level of dressage you are working at, almost all exercises appropriate to that level will help develop them, as long you keep the Scales uppermost in your mind as you do the exercise.

When starting to train a horse who is reasonably obedient and trustful, whether it is for dressage, eventing or show jumping, you should concentrate on the first three scales–rhythm, suppleness and contact.

RHYTHM

This first Scale is important for doing things well in any aspect of life; in dancing of course, but also in everything from typing, running and painting to walking and singing. I like the quote: 'Wisdom is discerning the true rhythm to things,' and that certainly applies in riding. So what is the rhythm we are looking for in the horse?

REGULARITY

Firstly we are looking for the horse to move in the rhythm that is natural to him.

THE WALK

In the walk the rhythm is a four-time marching beat. If you walk a horse down the road you will hear the four beats with equal intervals between each one. When you ride him, if you have learnt to follow the movement, you will feel first one seat bone being moved forward by his hind leg on that side, then the other by the hind leg on the opposite side. In front, his head will nod and to keep a good rhythm to the walk your hands need to follow this.

THE TROT

The trot is a two-time beat. The legs move in diagonal pairs, instead of separately as in the walk. As each diagonal pair leaves the ground it bounces the horse into a short moment when he is suspended in the air. Some horses who are badly trained and lose their natural spring simply step from one diagonal to the next. They still have a two-beat trot but they lose this moment of suspension that gives the trot expression.

Stages in the walk are shown in the photographs opposite. In the first picture the right hind and fore are forming a V, despite the pony spooking. The V formation by each lateral pair is a good indicator that the sequence is correct. Then an instant later he has relaxed, the near fore is lifting and when it returns to the ground the near hind will lift to enable the left hind and fore to form the same V shape as the right pair in the first picture.

The photographs above and below show the steps in the trot. The horse swings from one diagonal pair to the next.

THE CANTER

The canter is a three-beat gait and is different from the walk and trot because one side leads. You can see the foreleg on one side landing ahead of the foreleg on the other, and the hind leg on the same side slightly ahead of the one on the outside. Having a leading leg makes it easier for the horse to turn in that direction and, until he is well trained, rather uncomfortable, to turn to the other in what is known as counter canter.

The canter has a springing motion. We can start in the uphill moment (in which the horse looks good in the photographs). This is when the outside hind, only, is on the ground after the moment of suspension. Then a more horizontal moment as the diagonal pair (inside hind and outside fore) return and for a short time there are three legs on the ground before the outside hind thrusts off. The downhill tendency is when the leading leg returns, and after the diagonal pair thrust off, is the only one on the ground. Finally it too lifts off for another moment of suspension.

It's a lot of movement to follow when the horse is working in a good athletic canter. With all of this happening so quickly some riders do not follow it but tend to squash the natural spring. Then there is no clear moment of suspension and there is a tendency towards four beats.

Remember you are aiming to keep and even improve the horse's natural ability. Maintaining a good clear three-beat to the canter is very important. Have another look at the chapter on Following the Movement.

So these are the rhythms—the beats we want in each pace: a four-beat walk, two-beat trot and

The photographs opposite and above show the steps in the sequence of the canter and the changes in the steps from the uphill one to the downhill one and then moment of suspension.

three-beat canter. They are the correct rhythms for each pace and the official jargon found on the dressage sheet is that the paces are regular. If you ask dressage judges what is the most important factor in dressage, the majority will say regularity. This is because it is the key part of what is natural to the horse and what we must not spoil when we ride him. An irregular walk, trot or canter is a big mark-loser in dressage tests.

TEMPO

Another very important aspect of the rhythm is speed. You see horses trotting in a good clear two-beat, but one is racing around very fast and the other is going very slowly. They have different tempos to their rhythm.

FINDING THE BEST TEMPO

One of the most important aspects of dressage is finding the tempo in which the horse works best. It may change from day to day, but we want to find a speed in the trot where the horse has time to get in the air and show a moment of suspension but is not going so slowly that he is struggling and lazy. At each horse's individual best tempo he will find it easier to stay balanced and will show off the quality of his trot. The same with the canter. If you ask him to go quickly he will tend to get tight and tense; if too slowly he will get lazy and lose his three beat. You have to find the speed that is best for him.

KEEPING THE SAME TEMPO

The other important thing is to keep the same tempo when shortening and lengthening the strides. Lots of riders when they try to get their horse to lengthen the strides just make him go more quickly and there is none or very little extension. Similarly, when collecting the strides they slow down. In dressage we want to keep the same tempo—the one in which we have found the horse is most balanced—and this then helps to keep him relaxed and supple. It means no slowing down or speeding up whether we are going around turns, asking for forwards sideways work, lengthening or shortening the steps.

Keeping the same tempo is a big challenge for the rider.

Check List

Build up clear images of horses working in a good rhythm at walk, trot and canter.

Find the best tempo for your horse in each gait.

Keep that same tempo in all the work— no slowing down or speeding up.

SUPPLENESS

When we look at a human athlete running, jumping or doing gymnastics, the muscles work freely, contracting and relaxing, as is their job. The joints are mobile, helping this freedom, but at the same time there is strength and control. This is what we want from our horses, and ourselves (*Following the Movement* Chapter 2). This is the all-important second Training Scale that we call suppleness.

Often we make our horses obedient but do not worry about making their bodies as efficient as possible and developing their full athletic potential. A horse might work with a light contact (be willing) but it feels and looks like you are sitting on a board and the strides are tight and short. Another horse might be nervous, and keep shying or bucking; there is then no hope of getting the muscles to relax and work; he is too tense. In both cases we need to work on the suppleness, and as for the rider, this suppleness is determined by both the body and the mind.

For the horse to be supple he has to be made physically capable of using his body well and mentally relaxed enough so that he does not tighten through fear and tension.

The test that the horse is supple is that when you yield the reins, as in the free-rein walk, he will stretch forward and down and neither stay in the same position nor lift his head and neck.

The most important proof of good training is that the horse is able to move freely through his back; that the back is supple and swinging; and that he will stretch forward and down towards the bit whenever allowed to do so. If your training tightens and fixes the muscles in the horse's back you are not doing him justice and he will not jump or move as well as nature provided. His talents are not being used.

Check List

When a horse is supple:

His back will swing softly, like our hips (See *Following the Movement* page 25).

He will be comfortable to ride.

His hind legs will swing forward (not just up and down).

His tail will swing freely (not clamped down).

He will be good in the hand with an elastic feel through the rein (neither leaning or not taking the contact), and the mouth will have foam that shows it is champing softly (not opening wide or crossing the jaw).

Those are good things to aim for in your training!

Willingness to stretch forward and down when the rider allows the horse to take the reins out of his hands is a great test of whether the horse is working with suppleness.

CONTACT

Since you first started to ride you will have had some sort of contact between your hands and the bit. To be a dressage rider you have to aim for a contact that will make the horse more of an athlete. Any pulling back on the reins leads to less athleticism, because (a) he will tend to resist this type of contact and (b) it restricts the forward swing of the hind legs.

The contact we want as our goal is not one we make with the hands, as then we tend to pull back or see saw with our hands. It is contact made with our legs; and when we have reached the stage of being able to follow the movement, with our seat as well. This contact encourages the hind legs to be more active, to swing forward under the body and for the activity that it generates to go forward through the supple swinging back, free neck, into the mouth where it is felt through the reins by the rider's hands.

Diagram showing how the contact is made by the hind legs pushing forward and the activity generated going through the body to be felt in the rider's hands.

Thus the hands receive the contact that was generated by the use of the rider's legs (and seat) and they can do what they want with it. They can allow the horse to go more forward; they can restrain so that the horse collects; or they can guide the horse into a turn or movement. This is the ideal and takes time and training to establish, but we must keep it as our goal and work towards it if we want our happy athlete.

Firstly you have to provide receiving and allowing hands for the horse. (See page 11) Keep a consistent contact with the mouth; the fingers closed but not clamped on the reins; no pull-backs and no bending of the head from side to side. Then develop the feel that it is the driving aids that make the contact, not the hands. (See diagram on this page).

Ride your horse *forward into the contact.* This is the term I use more often than any other when I am judging. So few riders train their horses to work forward from behind into the contact. Most ride from the hands backwards into the hind quarters, so the hind legs are blocked from swinging forward and engaging.

N.B. The forward riding needed produces more active strides, not faster ones. Remember to keep the optimum tempo.

> ### Check List
>
> Aim for a consistent, light, elastic contact with the horse's mouth.
>
> Establish this contact by using your driving aids and riding forward into the contact.

FIRST PHASE

Rhythm, Suppleness, and Contact are the three goals you work towards when your horse and/or yourself first start dressage training. They are the goals in the first, confidence-building stages of dressage training. If you can establish them and then can keep them pretty well through transitions and turns, you are ready for the easier dressage tests You are also ready to start looking at the next two Scales of Training.

Remember that you will need to work on these three same scales as you advance up the grades in dressage. As you progress you will ask for a higher degree of rhythm, suppleness and contact, and even if you reach Grand Prix, you will be still working on them.

Swinging forward well with active hind legs.

on the soft side and a lighter one on the hard side. At the same time work on developing a bend around your inside leg on circles and serpentines, and make this bend as equal as possible to both sides (figures-of-eight are good for this).

The real straightening can be done when you put impulsion into the horse. This straightening is a never-ending task. Even fully trained horses will not by themselves work straight. The hard and soft sides might change but the rider will have to keep working on getting the hind legs to step forwards equally.

Check List

Real straightening comes from making both hind legs take equally forward-thrusting steps.

Ride your horse forward and make him straight.

Straightening the horse by fiddling with the reins can spoil the rhythm, suppleness and contact.

The photograph left shows a horse that is crooked with the quarters in. Above, the horse is absolutely straight.

The photograph opposite is a great illustration of collection. In this canter-pirouette the inside hind is stepping actively underneath the weight. It takes great strength from the horse and clear understanding between horse and rider. To achieve such quality to the work takes years of training and skillful riding.

COLLECTION

This is what dressage riders aim for: horses that can collect, that become more mobile, controllable, lighter and able to do very difficult movements. It is the ability to transfer the weight from the forehand, where it tends to fall when the horse is first ridden or trained poorly, back onto the hind quarters. This enables the horse to take shorter, higher steps, but without losing power.

There is just as much impulsion in the collected steps as in the extended ones. Many riders think of collecting simply as shortening the steps, so they slow the horse down and lose the power—this is a big mistake!

Collection takes good training over a long time, as the horse needs both to establish the earlier training scales to achieve it, and to build up the strength so that the hind quarters can take more weight.

Collection starts in the early stages of training. It happens whenever the weight is transferred backwards, as in any good downward transition, even with novice horses. So if you come into a halt and the horse engages and does not leave his hind legs behind him he is starting to collect.

Check List

Collection is transferring the weight from the forehand onto the hind quarters, to be able to shorten and heighten the steps without losing impulsion.

It is a gradual process starting with good transitions and ultimately leading to piaffe.

THROUGHNESS AND SELF-CARRIAGE

You might come across two important terms among the comments on your judges' sheets. These are basic concepts associated with all the Scales, and although barely recognisable in the novice horse become increasingly obvious in the well-trained horse as he progresses up the levels. Throughness is the sensitivity of the horse to the aids, so that he reacts immediately to them and the effect of them goes 'through' his entire body. Any resistance, tension, or blocking of the muscles stops the horse working 'through'.

Self-carriage is the ability of the horse to carry himself in the position that will help his body to work athletically: i.e. head in front of or on the vertical and taking enough weight on the hind quarters to stay balanced. He should also be balanced so that he can stay in this position without relying on support from the rider by, for example, leaning on the reins. Self-carriage is not a fixed outline. A horse can be in self-carriage when he is stretching and his head close to the ground, or when he has a high head and neck carriage in a very collected movement. The important points are that he is balanced and carrying himself.

CHAPTER 6
THE FIGURES

The figures are the various shapes asked for in tests, and by riding them in your training you also help to develop the Scales of Training. They all involve turning.

TURNING

The important points are that the horse:

• Keeps the rhythm so that there is no loss of balance. No speeding up or slowing down

• Shows that he is supple bending along the line of the turn and equally to both directions. The bend needs to be uniform along the length of his body: a flowing curve (no angles). The hind legs step into the tracks of the forelegs: no drifting out or in. The bend is around the rider's inside leg (the approximate centre of the horse) and not at the withers (too far forward to keep the uniform bend). Also, the bend is the same in both directions. He should be equally supple to both sides—but although you should always be

working towards this ideal, you can be reassured that it is very difficult to achieve. Even Grand Prix horses can show differences when turning from one way to the other.

• The contact is consistent with the horse stepping forward into it. The outside rein keeps a secure contact that controls the amount of bend in the neck. This helps to stop the outside shoulder drifting out. The inside rein is used for occasional softening, but is light and can be released without the horse losing his balance and positioning.

Turning starts by asking for flexion (see page 48). This has a softening effect and it is a good warning to the horse that something is about to happen. The uniform bend around the inside leg can then be asked for. As the bend is uniform along the length of the horse's body, the horse has to be very supple if he is to bend along the line of, say, an 8-metre circle, but is almost straight when on the line of a 20-metre circle.

That is why the first tests have big circles when little bend is needed and the more advanced ones smaller circles when the horse needs to be really supple.

You might be able to turn your novice horse in an 8-metre circle but you will only be able to do it by pulling on the inside rein. The horse is likely to slow down, lose his balance, stiffen and go against the contact. This is not going to help his way of going or contribute to his future as a dressage horse.

Remember turning by pulling the inside rein results in a bend in the neck and a blocking of the forward movement of the inside hind.

TURNS

A turn is quarter of a circle. There are plenty of turns in a dressage test, every corner is one and sometimes a movement asks for a turn right or left. For most novice horses one aims for a quarter of a circle with a 10-metre diameter; for ponies and elementary horses about 8-metres; and advanced horses 6-metres. The good rider will find the size with which the horse can cope and keep the Training Scales. It is important to prepare the horse for the turn with a half-halt and some softening to get a flexion to the inside-then, placing a little more weight in the inside stirrup, direct him forwards from behind with the legs and seat. If done well the turn will actually help to balance the horse and set him up for the next movement. If done badly he will lurch out of the turn onto his forehand; or his quarters may well stay to the inside of the track because the inside hind leg is not thrusting forward as

Turning onto the centre line in a good balance with the horse's body following the line of the curve.

Too much bend in the neck in this turn, and as the inside hind is stepping sideways not forwards, the weight and the power will be going out of the left shoulder.

much as the outside one. You have to use plenty of inside leg to encourage that lazy hind to work correctly.

Avoid making the turn too sharp or even pulling the horse into the corner with the outside rein because you think it is important to ride deep into the corners. Riding deep into the corners does give you more room to manoeuvre in the arena and is something to aim for, but your horse has to be really supple to go deep into a corner and keep the Scales. If you sacrifice the rhythm, suppleness and contact in order to do a deep turn, you will be losing many more marks than you gain, and you will not be developing a good way of going. So even if it means cutting the corners, keep to those Scales of Training. If you train your horse well you will progressively be able to ride deeper and deeper into the corners.

Turning with the wrong bend. The horse has tightened through the neck and lost his balance.

EXERCISES

Instead of the quarter-circle of the turn do a complete circle, so that at every corner you come to do a 10-metre circle. This helps to develop the feel of the horse bending around your leg in the turn, balancing on the outside rein (not the inside) and keeping the uniform bend.

In the trot about 3 metres before you start the turn, do a trot/walk/trot transition. This helps to develop the idea of half-halting in preparation for the turn.

As soon as you have completed a turn in the trot do a trot/walk/trot transition to help him balance and not fall onto the forehand.

After completing the turn, ride forward into some medium strides to help the horse straighten when he is tending to leave the quarters in.

Check List

Your position is really important. Stretch upwards and turn your shoulders to follow those of the horse and the line of the turn.

Prepare.

Keep the inside leg and the outside rein as the dominant aids, not the inside rein.

CIRCLES

These are a development of the turn and in them you have more time to get the horse really swinging forward towards the bit and showing off his athleticism. It is said that if you can ride a circle well, you are a proper dressage rider. Circles are not easy, especially as they get smaller.

As usual, the first thing is to keep the Training Scales. To do that you follow the same ideas as in the turn–preparation, positioning yourself; inside leg and outside rein dominant; inside rein just for softening; direct him forward from behind with your legs and seat.

Then you have to ride the correct shape and size. The 20-metre circles are relatively easy as you only have to turn a small amount each stride and the four key points of the circle will be quite clear as the arena is 20 metres wide (see diagram on this page). It often helps to think of the circle as diamond shaped, so you ride towards one point. Before, not when, arriving at each of these points start aiming for the next point. When a 15-metre or 10-metre circle is asked for you need to look at the arena and decide where the four points are going to be, and watch others riding the circles.

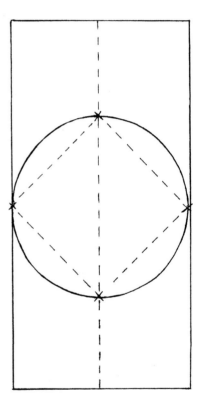

The circle showing how to ride for the four points.

THE SERPENTINE

This is a great figure for making your horse more supple and seeing whether he can keep the same rhythm through the turns. It is also a good one to test whether the rider can keep upright in the turns, follow the turning horse, and not collapse when going in one or both directions. The serpentine is a series of loops (usually three but can be four or five). Each time you cross the centre line you should have a straight horse, but in the turn he should be bent along the line of the turn. To get a good result, you really need to help your horse keep his balance, half-halting when he speeds up, asking for more forwardness when he slows down. You have to think well ahead, preparing early enough to enable him to show that he is supple in both directions.

To have him straight on the centre line you need to be asking for straightness at the end of the turn. To have him bent for the turn, you need to prepare for the next direction before crossing the centre line, putting slightly more weight in the new inside stirrup, and softening to get a little flexion. Then as you cross the centre line turning yourself and the horse into the new direction.

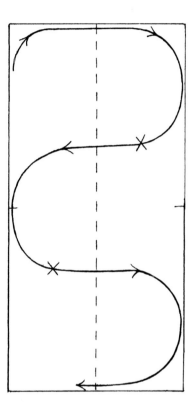

A Serpentine.. The Xs show where preparations are made to establish the new flexion and bend.

LOOPS

Loops are performed in trot, and quite often in canter as an easy start for counter-canter. The principles are similar to the serpentine, but there are fewer changes of bend.

In the trot the horse once again follows the line and is bent accordingly. He is prepared and turned off the track in the same bend that he turned the corner. Before turning back to the track and reaching the required 3, 5 or 8 metres depth of the loop, prepare him for the change of bend, then change the bend. Similarly, just before reaching the track, prepare and then change the bend back into the original one. Remember, too, you need only as much bend as to follow the line; for a 3-metre loop this is barely any.

In the canter keep him flexed towards his leading leg throughout the loop. The important point is to ride him forward to keep the clear three beat of the canter and to keep the hind legs on the line of the loop (it is easy for them to drift off it). This takes a rider with a good secure balanced seat who is not relying on the inside rein for turning, but directs the horse forward along the line of the loop with legs and seat.

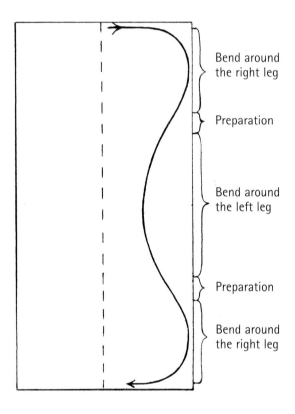

Bend around the right leg

Preparation

Bend around the left leg

Preparation

Bend around the right leg

Diagram of a Loop

CHAPTER 7
THE KEY MOVEMENTS

The dressage movements are both tests of how well, and to what level, the Scales of Training have been established; also they are a way of improving the Scales of Training. The movements start from the very simple, such as a halt or a transition into trot, and they progress to very difficult ones, that need a high degree of collection, great understanding between horse and rider, and years of training to develop the strength to be able to do them. The ultimate movements for a competition horse are piaffe and passage and for the High School horses at places like the Spanish Riding School, the Airs Above the Ground.

Some ponies and some young people have done these very difficult movements but in this short book we are going to focus on the movements that you will come across in the Pony Club, Preliminary, Novice and Elementary tests in Britain and Training and First levels in the USA.

In competitions, the way in which a movement is performed tells the judges how supple a horse is and whether he can maintain rhythm and contact.

In training, the movements are carried out to make the horse more supple, define the rhythm, make the contact more secure, develop impulsion, and get him straighter. So movements are very important: not so much in terms of achieving the technical requirements, but both as a test and a means of improving the Training Scales.

The primacy of the Training Scales is a mindset that riders, judges and trainers find very hard to adhere to. Most think of movements rather than the Training Scales as the measure of success and that makes it so much more difficult to produce a happy athlete and for the ambitious to succeed at an international level.

When you are carrying out a movement, whether it is a transition from trot to walk, or shoulder-in, think less about ending up square, or achieving the required angle, and more about keeping the rhythm, suppleness, contact, etc. If you take care of these and do the right preparations, the movement will happen almost for itself.

Check List

Never stop thinking about Rhythm, Suppleness, Contact
(and as you advance Impulsion, Straightness, Collection). These are more important than the technical requirements of a movement.

THE TRANSITIONS

Transitions are the changes from one pace to another and within the pace from one form of it to another (e.g. working trot to medium trot). They are the most important movements because:

- They are the most numerous movements. Look at a test and count how many transitions there are in it.
- They are the best indicator of how well the Scales of Training have been achieved: i.e. how well the horse has been trained.
- They are the most useful movements for developing engagement, reaction to aids, and all the Scales of Training when training the horse.

These are pretty overwhelming credentials, so you need to learn how to do them well. Poor transitions will lose you many marks in a test and will not help you to train the horse better. What do you look for in a good transition?

- Training Scales.
- Fluency.
- Rhythm of pace maintained up to the moment that there is a change of pace: i.e. no slowing down or speeding up before the transition.
- Rhythm of pace maintained for transitions within a pace: i.e. no speeding up into mediums, or slowing down into working/collection.
- Hind quarters engage in downward transitions.
- Hind quarters push off in upward transitions.

This picture shows how much better it is to make a transition without pulling on the reins. With a light contact the horse is able to step well under the weight with his hind legs in the transition to walk.

We have looked at the basics of transitions in Chapter 4 (page 42) The horse has learnt that a check on the rein and a soothing voice-aid mean a downward transition; and a squeeze/kick and a click or chirpy voice-aid mean an upward transition. He is obedient and may be able to fulfill the technical requirement and do the transition wherever it may be asked for, but it will be quite difficult for him to keep the Scales. He will need more help if he is to keep his balance, not stick his head in the air, elongate, lean on the bit, start to run or slow down. This is where you have to co-ordinate your aids and use them to give him the support he needs to keep the rhythm, suppleness and contact.

THE DOWNWARD TRANSITION

A non-allowing aid on the outside rein starts the downward transition. On straight lines from walk and trot both hands can be used: otherwise the outside rein dominates. The legs are used in a supportive way rather than actively. Stretch up, tighten the back, as described in *The Collecting Effect* (Chapter 3 page 37) and think of the movement that the lower back will follow in the next pace. Ideally the rein-aid is simply a non-allowing aid: the fingers close on the rein and the arm tightens (does not pull back), but if not effective then the voice and a series of checks may be necessary.

Losing balance and going above the bit in the transition.

After thousands of downward transitions achieved through using the same clear aids the horse gradually learns to react more quickly and with lighter and lighter aids. With a well-trained horse the rider can ask for a downward transition simply by sitting up. But if anything goes wrong, the good rider is ready to apply the appropriate aid: i.e. the rein if the horse runs on, the leg if he slows down or does not engage etc.

The photograph right shows the horse losing balance again but this time leaning on the bit, and going onto the forehand in the transition.

In the pictured below, the horse is keeping a better balance.

What can go wrong?

• *The horse can fall onto the forehand and lean on the reins.*
The way forward: Transfer more weight onto the hind quarters. Make sure the horse is well engaged and working forward into a light elastic contact before asking for the transition. Check you are sitting upright and not being pulled forward. Give good support with legs. Check that hands are held above withers and not below it. Lift inside hand six inches or so as ask for transition.

• *The horse can stick his head in the air.*
The way forward: Build up greater security in the contact. Ride more forward into the contact before asking for transition so that the horse is better connected between hind legs and bit. Check not pulling back in the transition with horse resisting against this. Check main aid is outside, not inside rein. Ask for transition when on 8-10metre circle (in trot) 12–15-metre (in canter) and use outside rein (inside rein ONLY for softening).

• *The horse can hollow and lose engagement.*
The way forward: Horse is tightening and hollowing his back, so concentrate on making it more supple and working through it. Use exercises to make the horse more supple before the transition (circles, serpentine, riding positively forward into contact). Check that your weight is not making him hollow and that you can take some weight out of the saddle by putting more into the thighs and the stirrups. Give good support with the legs during the transition.

• *The horse can slow down but does not change pace (common in the canter/trot transition).*
The way forward: This is usually due to too much reliance on the inside rein that blocks the inside hind leg from stepping through to establish the new pace. Try flexing or even bending the horse to the outside. Think of lifting the inside rein or opening it so it is away from the horse's neck (Chapter 4 page 45). Apply aid with the outside rein only. Make sure that horse is not tight in back. Make him more supple and swinging through it with plenty of forward-going work, and a light seat.

• *The horse shortens his neck and his nose gets closer to his chest.*
The way forward: This usually means that the horse is not responding to the rein-aids and the rider is pulling with his reins to get a response. The horse has to be made more obedient. Use checks—momentary strong applications of the reins, particularly on the outside one, and use your voice. As soon as he responds, allow with the reins and actually give with the inside one, so for a short time there is no contact on it.

• *The horse's quarters swing to one side.*
The way forward: Check not using opposite rein more strongly; pulling on left rein will make quarters swing to right. Give more support with legs and perhaps hold them a little further back. Check that you are sitting square in the saddle and weight is not drifting to one side.

EXERCISES

Watch a horse and rider making good transitions and keep this image clearly in your mind when you ride transitions yourself on your own horse. It is amazing how much you absorb by watching. Working to an image, you do not have to try hard or think of everything you should be doing, all of which tends to make you tight and stiff and inhibits a good transition.

Leg-yielding, or thinking leg-yielding can help to make the horse supple and working into the outside rein, so do this for a few strides before and even during the transition.

Make the transitions on a circle, as this helps the horse to be supple (key to good transitions) and encourages rider to use the outside rein for the aid and the inside one only for softening.

Check List

Make your horse obedient with checks (remember only apply for one stride, but can repeat) and with the voice before trying to co-ordinate the aids.

Make your horse supple and accepting a good contact before you ask for the transition.

Stretch up, support with legs and apply a non-allowing contact with the outside rein dominating.

THE UPWARD TRANSITION

In the early upward transitions the horse will tend to lean on the bit and pull himself into the next pace. As he becomes stronger, more balanced with the weight being taken off the forehand, he can develop that all-important thrust of the hind legs to push him into the next pace. The forward transitions then become wonderful tools to make him stronger in the hind quarters and able to spring off into the next

Below and opposite: series showing the transition to canter where the rider has held hard with the inside rein in the first picture. This has restricted the horse's power to get into the canter and he loses his balance: proving how quickly things can change, he is in a good canter moments later.

pace. To get the hind legs to work in this way compressing them a little so that they can thrust off, they need plenty of messages from the rider's legs to become active and really work. It is not just a matter of giving these aids when you are ready to make the transition, but of preparing the horse so that he has the power to obey your commands.

From the halt he needs a warning that he is about to be asked to go forward: a softening aid on the reins and then the legs by the girth.

In the walk he needs to be actively marching forward to the bit if he is to get into the trot smoothly and fluently.

The trot needs to be full of power if he is to be able to get into the canter, and there is the added problem of wanting him to strike off onto a particular leading leg. You have to make it clear to him which one you want by flexing him in the direction of the leading leg. It is really important to use a softening aid only with the inside rein. Any pulling back will stop the inside hind leg coming through and he will not be able to spring off into the canter. To encourage the inside hind leg to do its work, use your inside leg actively with plenty of changes in pressure. Make sure your weight is down on the inside stirrup as that is another help to getting him onto the right leg; but no leaning, as this is counter-productive and in fact transfers the weight to the outside. Another good indicator to the horse as to which leg to go off on is your outside leg, which should be taken backwards a little, and applied. Finally your outside rein needs to be the one that stops him from simply doing a faster trot. You have to regulate and balance him with this one.

What can go wrong?

• *The horse loses balance and sticks his head in the air.*

The way forward: This is usually due to the horse not having enough power to get into the next pace, so build up the activity. The trot/canter transition gives most people problems at the beginning. The usual reason for difficulties is that the horse simply does not have enough power in the trot to be able to get into the canter without losing his balance and sticking his head in the air. So make sure that you have plenty of impulsion in the trot. The second most common reason for difficulties in this transition is that the rider tries to get a bend to the inside, pulls back or at least restrains with the inside rein and this kills off the impulsion. Quite often it helps to go into the canter with a slight flexion to the outside if this is the cause of the problems.

• *The horse speeds up.*

The way forward: Often horses trot faster before getting into the canter. In the beginning this is not a serious problem, but as the training advances, stronger use of the outside rein should prevent this.

• *The horse strikes off on the wrong leg.*

The way forward: If this is a problem, riders often ask for a bigger and bigger bend to the inside, but this just makes it more difficult to step forward with the inside hind leg. Instead, think of getting the positioning by leg-yielding just before and even during the transition. Asking for a leg-yield into the outside rein: i.e. if you want a right lead, leg-yield to the left.

EXERCISES

Like the downward transitions work, make sure that the horse is going in a good rhythm, is supple and working to a good forward–feeling contact, before asking for a transition. Again, use circles and serpentines to achieve this.

Probably the most used exercise in the whole world of dressage helps to get a better trot/canter transition. Work on a 20-metre circle then spiral gradually in to a 10-metre circle with a bend around your inside leg that follows the line of the circle. Then leg-yield (page 100) back onto the 20-metre circle. Take great care to keep your weight in your inside leg; that your inside leg is active and by the girth; and that you keep the horse almost straight with just a slight flexion to the inside. This means that you only use the inside rein for softening, and the horse steps into the outside rein. The outside rein can be used to check occasionally in order to keep the horse straight. As you reach the 20-metre circle, ask for the canter. If you have applied the aids in this way it will make the transition very easy.

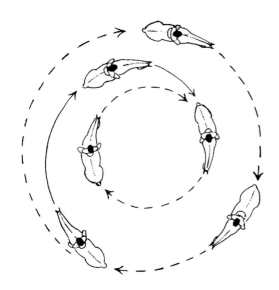

> **Check List**
>
> Prepare by establishing the rhythm, suppleness and contact.
>
> Build up the activity so that the horse has the power to change the pace.
>
> Make sure that you stay upright and do not lean forward.
>
> Use your aids to encourage the hind legs to be active and thrust off into the next pace.

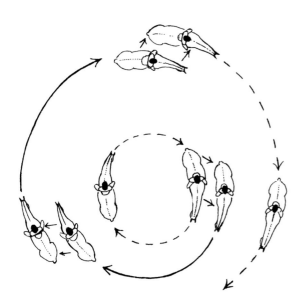

Diagram of Spiralling Circles

THE HALF-HALT

This was looked at from the rider's perspective on page 38. It is only half a transition, as you give the aids for the downward transition, but momentarily, so before changing pace the aids are released and for a second the rein contact eased. The result is that instead of a change of gear there is a containment of the power.

The half-halt is a key movement in dressage, as when performed well it has so many wonderful effects. To do it well is very difficult, taking a well trained horse with well-established Training Scales and a very balanced rider with subtle aids. As in most things in dressage, we can progress to or at least towards the ultimate from very simple beginnings.

The beginning of the half-halt is when you check the horse for no more than one stride. It becomes a little more effective when you keep the legs on at the same time, with supportive

aids. This stops the hind legs falling backwards and losing any engagement.

You see the show jumpers and event riders applying this sort of half-halt when they want to shorten the stride into a fence, or to balance their horse so he takes more weight on the quarters and will therefore have more power to jump a fence.

Quite often the head comes up when they make one of these checks. It does not matter: they are not after that good way of going sought in dressage, but just want to clear a fence. Checks would lose marks in dressage because they usually disturb the rhythm, create tension, and destroy the even contact. They are, however, useful in the early stages of training, and if more subtle control is lost!

In the half-halt, the rider encourages the hind legs to step forward under the body so that he uses his legs. He needs to stop this forward thrust from making the horse go faster, so he contains the horse with his non-allowing hands, followed

The aids applied for half-halt – containing the horse between the leg, back and hand aids for a moment. The results are seen in the second picture with more engagement and activity to the trot.

by a slight easing of the contact. This may have little effect at first, but the important thing is to make the horse react, not by keeping the aids on for longer, or making them stronger, but by applying them more frequently. As long as the aids are consistent and neither so long nor so strong that they disturb the rhythm, suppleness and contact, gradually over weeks and months the horse will start to react more. He will start to contain/collect his body, transfer a fraction more weight onto the hind quarters, lighten his forehand a tiny amount, and begin to accept the warning that a movement is about to be asked of him.

When he starts to accept these aids, and the back is getting stronger and able to swing freely in the trot-work, the leg and hands can be supported by the seat aids. A tightening of the rider's muscles, an upward stretch and momentarily stopping the lower back from following the horse's movement will encourage the hind quarters to engage. Any tendency by the horse to hollow and take his back away or to tighten means that the rider should revert to just using his legs. A half-halt will lose most of its value if the thrust from the hind leg is blocked from getting through to the bit and the rider's hands, because the horse hollows or tightens his back.

Over time as it becomes easier to maintain the Training Scales, you can support the legs and hands in the half-halt with the seat.

EXERCISES

The best exercise for both getting the horse to understand and for developing the half-halt is first to work on the trot/walk/trot transitions. Teach the horse to make the transition into the walk in a forward manner, with light rein-aids and stepping well under the weight with the hind legs. Then after a few steps of walk, ask him to thrust off with the hind legs into the trot. Working on a 20-metre circle, do plenty of these transitions over a number of training sessions. When confident that they are going well: in the trot, apply the aids to go to walk, but only momentarily, so there is no change of pace, just a short containment of the movement. It is little more than thinking of going to walk, with a tightening of your legs, back and arms, then a release. This is the half-halt. Remember that in the beginning you will feel little, but do not panic and apply longer and stronger aids. The way forward is through light, brief aids and hundreds no thousands of repetitions.

Check List

Start by establishing obedience to a check.

Then use leg and rein aids to contain the horse momentarily before the release.

When Training Scales maintained using these aids support with weight aids.

Teach through, repetition not by making aids stronger or longer.

A good half-halt is barely visible to the eye.

Good riders use hundreds of half-halts in a test.

CHAPTER 8
MORE MOVEMENTS

Most riders when they first start to teach a movement, whether it is a halt or shoulder-in, focus on the technical requirements. They rarely think about the preparation or about putting the horse in a position to carry out the movement easily; nor do they focus on keeping the Scales. The result is that the horse usually tightens and resists the contact: yet they go on applying the aids for the movement and are very pleased to think 'I have done a halt', or 'I can do shoulder-in'. In truth they are missing the essence of riding a movement.

The key factors in teaching and riding a movement are:

- Preparing the horse so that he flows into the movement.

- Keeping the Scales—rhythm, suppleness and contact at all times.

- Introducing the movement progressively so that when asking for a halt from a trot, first allow half a dozen strides of walk and do not worry whether the horse is straight or square. Or in leg-yield only ask for a very small amount of sideways movement. As the horse reacts well to the preparation and keeps the Scales, the demands can be increased and the technical requirements worked on. But never forget that good preparation and maintaining the Scales must always be uppermost in the rider's mind, **not** the technical requirements.

TURNING AROUND THE FOREHAND

This movement is not found in any tests, and its close relative the turn on the forehand very rarely. The aim of dressage is to take the horse off the forehand and it is therefore a movement used mostly in the early stages of training of both horse and rider. As a teaching-aid to both of them it is invaluable.

The turn around the forehand teaches the horse to yield and to step sideways away from

the inside leg of the rider; to step into the outside rein; and to stretch the all-important back muscles through taking these sideways steps. These are three key parts of training.

The movement teaches the rider even more because:

- To do it well the rider has to learn to stay balanced and central in the saddle despite a natural inclination to start pushing with the seat and to collapse the body in the effort to get the horse stepping around.

- The rider has to learn to co-ordinate the aids: to understand that the control comes from the outside rein when the natural inclination is to dominate with the inside rein. The inside rein is only there to soften and not to pull back. The dominating leg is the inside leg by the girth and is the one into which the weight is directed (not slipping to the outside), and finally the outside leg is a support but is only applied if the horse starts to turn around his centre instead of the fore-hand.

The turn around the forehand. The horse is making a big step sideways with the hind quarters. Because the rider is upright and controlling with the outside rein to keep the neck more or less straight, he is keeping the balance pretty well and not drifting into the big danger of a turn around the centre with a lot of crossing—falling onto the outside (left) shoulder.

All of this may be hard to master at first, but when done well it helps the rider to come to terms with some key concepts:

- The importance of the inside leg in producing a bend rather than the inside rein producing a hinge at the wither and a bend in the neck.

- Getting the horse to step into the outside rein by riding into it with the inside leg.

- Keeping the inside rein light.

- Lateral work (stepping sideways away from the leg).

- Keeping the horse balanced and upright when he steps sideways.

So spend time learning to do the turn correctly and then everything else will be so much easier.

It is a movement that can be done at the walk, and taken very slowly (a stride at a time): that gives the rider time to think about (a) what he should do and is doing, and (b) to stop and correct when necessary. To give the rider time to think about what lies ahead and to prepare, I like to start from the halt.

WHAT THE RIDER WANTS TO ACHIEVE:

The horse is almost straight, with just a slight inside flexion at the poll so the rider can see the inside eye. In this movement like leg-yielding and shoulder-in, the flexion is away from the direction in which the horse will move.

The horse steps sideways around the forehand with the inside hind leg crossing over the outside hind leg. The forelegs keep marching in the rhythm of the walk and describe a small circle; a small one in the turn on the forehand; and as large as you like for a turn around the forehand.

It is very important for there to be a forward tendency and no backward steps.

It is better to describe a bigger circle with the forelegs than to step back or to lose the Scales. The turn on the forehand is usually through 180 degrees.

WHAT THE RIDER DOES:

- Establishes a relaxed balanced halt.

- Takes his time to check his position, thinks of staying upright, stretching upwards and, without any leaning or slipping, puts the weight slightly down the inside leg that will ask for the sideways steps.

- Softens with the inside rein to establish a light elastic feel with the mouth and just enough flexion to see the inside eye.

- Applies the inside leg by the girth, not further back, as this will destroy so many of the benefits of the turn on the forehand. Aim for the feeling that the horse's ribs are yielding slightly and the inside hind crosses clearly over the outside one.

The outside rein controls the bend to ensure that there is no bend in the neck whatsoever. Also, little half-halts with this rein (momentary non-allowing pressure or if necessary a light check) will stop the horse moving forward and will also tend to help to the inside hind take a bigger step sideways.

Co-ordinating all these aids is not easy, but keep practicing because it will help you to become a much better rider.

A halt before asking for the turn is a good way to start. When you feel happy doing this in both directions and are sure you can keep the horse from bending in the neck and falling out of the outside shoulder, you can begin from the walk.

Turning around the forehand can be done on a much bigger circle when it becomes more like leg-yield, but the principles are the same: the most important ones being controlling the bend with the outside rein so that the horse does not fall onto the shoulder; and making him responsive to the inside leg by the girth, so that he steps across and loosens up his back muscles.

Remember not to go on asking for the same thing for too long. Keep changing direction and interspersing the turns with some trot work to get the hind legs engaged and active again. Also you do not have to keep to a 180-degree turn. You can do a trot/walk transition and then a few steps of turn around the forehand and back into the trot, or you can do a 360-degree turn with the front legs following a circle of about 10 metres diameter. These are all excellent suppling exercises when practised competently.

Check List

Take your time.

Keep upright.

Dominant aids are inside leg and outside rein.

Maintain Training Scales.

THE HALT

The requirements of the halt become progressively more demanding. So for a Grand Prix horse you would expect it to be absolutely square and straight, well engaged and with direct transitions in and out of it—somewhat tricky! In the easiest dressage tests you will get fairly good marks if the horse stays relaxed and still, and accepting the contact. For the higher marks the front legs need to be square and the hind quarters directly behind the front legs.

If you are going to train your horse to achieve better and better halts, the most important things is for him to be is relaxed in them and not to move so that he can remain supple and accepting the contact. Once you can keep your horse relaxed in the halt, you can start to work on achieving a higher degree of the technical requirements.

The other key factor in the halt is the transitions in and out. The problem with so many riders is that they 'jam on the brakes' into the halt. They ask by fixing their hands, quite often pulling back, sometimes leaning back and rarely supporting with the legs. Some horses are so obedient that they realise what is meant and come into a halt, but for most, these aids create all sorts of problems. The hands used in this way make the contact unpleasant, so there is resistance. Also, any pull-back forces the hind legs to drag rather than engage. Then leaning back is a driving-aid to go forward, so this is confusing to the horse and also tends to make him hollow his back.

In the top pic
the rider is appl
the aids for the h
containing the h
between the s
legs and hands
the second pict
just one stride l
a good halt has b
established, and
contact eased.

For a good transition into the halt use a repetition of the aids: a series of half-halts and an easing of them as soon as he is about to stop. It is also the preparation that makes these half-halts work best so the horse needs to be in a good rhythm, supple, and working to an even contact before they are applied.

For horse and rider who have only just started their dressage training, aim first and foremost to make the transitions fluent and this will mean making them progressive. From the trot give your series of half-halts to go forward into the walk; and then in the walk give a few more light half-halts until the horse stops.

Out of the halt be positive but gentle with your forward-driving aids and allow him to take one or two walk steps to help him keep balanced and straight. Gradually as your horse becomes more responsive and balanced you can reduce the number of walk steps.

EXERCISES

If he is getting unbalanced and hollowing into the halt, apply the aids for the turn around the forehand as you come down from the trot, and take up to one step sideways. Change the direction of the sideways steps each time.

If he is running on into the halt and you have to use strong rein-aids try to find an area to work him where there is a high wall, fence or hedge. Then do a figure-of-eight but with an extra long straight stretch in between the two 10- to 15-metre circles.

After you have done a few figures-of-eight when you are approaching the straight stretch with the barrier ahead of you, apply the aids for a halt. If he does not respond, keep him straight and let him head into the barrier, where he will have to stop. Pat him and start the exercise again. Keep repeating it until you can get him responding better to your aids.

Keep this up for a few training sessions, then do the exercise on the centre line with the figure-of-eight using X as the centre. At X ask for the halt. If it works reasonably well, repeat it a few times; if it does not, return to working in front of your barrier. Pat your horse as soon as he responds, and give him frequent breaks. Never work on the same exercise for too long in any one training session, but return to it one or two days later.

Progress to coming straight down the centre line and asking for the halt. Whenever you are unhappy with the results, return to doing the halt in the centre of a figure-of-eight.

STRETCHING

This is the best test of whether the horse is supple; taking a forward feeling contact; and thrusting forwards with the hind legs so that the power goes through the back and neck and is received and contained by the hands through the reins (see diagram on page 58). It means that when the rider loosens his grip on the reins with his fingers and allows the horse to take as much rein as he wants, the horse is keen to do so and stretches forwards and down. He keeps the same rhythm (does not lose his balance and fall onto his forehand) and the back remains supple with the muscles relaxing and contracting freely.

The most common form of this stretching asked for in the tests is the free walk on a long rein when the horse marches boldly forward and takes that contact forward and down. In some of the new tests it is asked for in the trot and occasionally the canter. For judges this stretching helps them to assess whether the horse is working correctly, and for the rider it is a very important part of training.

Why you should stretch your horse often:

• When muscles get tired they become painful. Most horses will react to the pain by resisting and tightening. Many riders do not understand this and think that it is willful disobedience, so they battle to obtain submission. If the horse is allowed to stretch, every 10 minutes or so, all of this is avoided. When you are training or riding-in at shows, give your horse frequent breaks, allow him to stretch (but keep him active) in the walk or trot.

• Back muscles need to operate freely, not to tighten, as they are the ones that help the horse to move correctly and freely. Stretching of the muscles helps them to develop and to remove any blocks that might be building up. Working in a stretched outline is very important, particularly when the horse first starts each work session and may be a bit stiff, and in the early stages of the dressage training. It is the best way of getting the all-important back muscles to operate.

Stretching well, staying balanced and active.

Stretching in the walk in a free walk on a long rein. This a really good way of allowing the horse to ease his muscles in a work session without letting him become lazy.

To get a horse to stretch:

- A horse will stretch because his muscles are working freely and he is supple. If there is tension; if he works in a fixed outline; if his back is hollow and stiff, he will not stretch, so you need to work on these to get the stretching—making him more relaxed in his mind, more supple in his body.

- A horse will stretch because he works forward into the contact and likes the feel he has with the rider's hands. When the rider eases this contact he will stretch forward to try and establish it again. If the rider has any backward tendency in his hands, if the horse is held into an outline, if the hind legs are being dragged or just going up and down without swinging forward and thrusting then the horse will not stretch. You need to work on these to achieve the stretching: develop a forward feeling contact and a more forward way of going (long thrusting strides not quick short ones).

EXERCISES

Use exercises such as serpentines, circles, canter/trot/canter, turning around the forehand, leg-yielding, to progressively make the horse more and more supple.

Use the spiralling circles (Key Movements, Transitions page 79) and returning to the outer circle with leg-yielding steps to develop a good forward-feeling contact on the outside rein. When you reach the outer circle for the first few times, freshen up the trot with some longer strides to develop the forward thrust. When this is going well, on the next occasion when you reach the outer circle allow the horse to stretch, making sure that the inside rein is almost loose and that it is the outside one that keeps that very very light but unrestricted contact.

Note of caution

Stretching forward and down does not mean allowing the horse to fall onto the forehand. It means stretching the top-line muscles and lightening the load on the shoulder rather like when a horse jumps in really good style, bending his back, dropping his head and basculing over the fence. You must keep him active, but relaxed, with the weight on the hind quarters—so do not take it as your rest-time or lean forward.

Check List

Make sure that he is supple: perhaps using a little flexion left and then right, and holding each flexion for a few strides.

Allow the horse to take the reins out of your hands, and—if on a circle—particularly the inside rein.

Keep yourself upright and keep the horse active but relaxed.

Keep the rhythm: don't allow any speeding up or slowing down.

Changing from a medium trot (above) into a collected one (below) without losing the power or cadence.

DEVELOPING THE MEDIUM PACES

When the horse is working in a trot or canter that he finds most natural and that is relatively easy for him to stay balanced, it is known as the 'working' trot or canter. The important point in the working paces is to find the tempo that allows him to show off the pace at its best. If you race around, he will get tight and take short steps; if you go too slowly he will just become lazy and not develop power or swing. Finding the speed that suits the horse is an important rider skill.

The next stage is to be able to get him to lengthen his strides, but without changing the tempo. Only lengthening is asked for, not speeding up. To do this takes power, and until he has it, he will tend to quicken and run onto his forehand. You have to make the hind legs active so that they thrust forwards to give the horse the power to lengthen his steps. Then he has to be supple, with his back swinging so that the muscles can do their work and help the horse to lengthen his strides.

The horse will find it easy to produce medium strides if he is both strong enough to generate power with his hind quarters and is supple. First you have to develop his strength in the hind quarters largely through well-performed transitions and good active working paces, but this takes time. Only the super-talented horse produces medium strides when he is first trained. Secondly, and at the same time, you have to develop his suppleness through serpentines, circles, turning around the forehand, leg yielding and so on.

When he has the strength and is able to engage his hind quarters he can be asked for some medium strides, but it is not just a matter of applying the aids: you have to prepare him so that he has the ability to lengthen. You have to set him up with half-halts; have a good rhythm; make sure he is supple; establish a good forward feeling contact and encourage him to push off and not drag his hind legs.

Remember: every pull that you make on the reins stops the hind legs from stepping forward by much more than the amount you pull back. Keep referring to the section on allowing hands,

Above and opposite: opening the horse out into the longer frame and strides of the medium canter.

on pages 11 and 15.

Finally, when you ask for strides with the driving aids remember that the strides should be become longer but not faster. It is important to do this progressively, at first only asking for a slight lengthening and for only a few strides, and, as it begins to feel good, asking for a little more. I like to do this on a circle, starting with trot/walk/trot transitions, then trot/canter/trot transitions, and then a few medium strides.

What is really important is not to relax when you have done some good medium strides but to return to the working pace with a good transition. Ride him forward into the shorter

working strides without slowing down: then you are retaining and developing the power that you can use for the next medium strides. This means using your legs to keep him active behind, containing with the outside rein, and softening but not blocking with the inside one.

Ask more frequently for these vital transitions: working/medium/working. Gradually, over time, develop better and better medium, but at first be satisfied with very little.

Then progress to asking for medium strides across diagonals or on the longside, but remember that the horse will only produce the medium if he is supple and has the power to do so. Use the short side to develop these.

In the medium trot, to help keep the horse's back supple and swinging it is usually best to start in rising trot, or at least be ready to go into rising trot if he tightens at all during the medium.

To develop a good medium canter he needs to be relatively straight. With the novice horse this can be difficult but do not worry about the quarters being in a little or the odd wobbles, but do give him every chance to be straight. Don't ask for medium before he is relatively straight, particularly when coming out of a corner: complete the turn and do not leave the quarters in as you ask for the medium. Work on getting the two hind legs to step forward equally. Check where your weight is: i.e. if your shoulder and seat position have helped to get a complete turn and do not fiddle around with the reins in your effort to straighten him. Ride him positively forward.

Remember too that in both paces the transition into working is your chance to build up power, not the opportunity to relax and stop asking anything of your horse, or, worse, to stop him with the reins and ask him to slow down.

Check List

Prepare, prepare, prepare. This preparation covers both the weeks and months leading up to asking for medium paces (making him strong, engaged and supple enough), and the last few strides before asking for the medium (asking for more power with forward driving half-halts and checking on the suppleness) (page 56).

Apply the driving aids.

Stretch up and feel as if you are encouraging the horse's shoulders to lift.

It is better to produce less lengthening and to keep the rhythm for then the horse will stay more relaxed and supple. This is a better basis for future improvement. Half-halt if he starts to run, give more driving aids if he slows down.

In the downward transition keeping the power is all-important—only let your horse shorten his steps, no slowing down.

Be satisfied with small bytes of progress—it takes time.

EXERCISES

The spiralling circles help again (page 79). Ask for the medium when you return to the outer circle. You can do this in both the trot and the canter, but in the canter you always stay on one track even when returning to the outer circle—no leg yielding.

Doing some counter-canter and a good forward transition into the trot helps develop the medium trot. Go for the medium as soon as you feel the horse is balanced enough after the transition. If he is able to do the counter-canter around the short side, make a transition to trot at the quarter-marker then into medium down the longside.

A good medium walk marching forward freely with an allowing contact.

THE MEDIUM WALK

This is different from the trot and canter as there is no working walk. The walk is a pace with no moment of suspension, so the horse does not have such scope within it to produce so many variations. I like to think of the medium walk as a free walk ridden with a contact that is light and unrestrictive so that the horse can march forward with supple, relaxed strides. The strides are almost as long as in the free walk, and it is the same speed for both: i.e. no slowing down of tempo when you take up a contact.

It is easy for a rider to spoil the correct rhythm of the walk if the rein contact is uneven; if he is holding back with the reins; or if the horse becomes tense and tightens his back. The four-time marching rhythm is easily lost through rider interference. It is best to keep mainly to a free-rein walk, and only use short sessions in the medium walk until the horse is well on in the training.

EXERCISES

Give your horse a good free walk on a long rein then gradually take up the contact BUT without any slowing down or shortening of the strides. This is a really good test of whether your contact is restrictive or allowing.

A series showing the simple change by a young pony to whom the rider is giving plenty of support with the legs and hands.

SIMPLE CHANGES

In the simple change, the horse is asked for a transition from canter to walk then to take a few steps in walk that show clearly that the walk is relaxed and four-time; and then to strike off directly into the canter but leading on the other leg.

In the canter-walk transition he has to make a big change in miles per hour from the canter, which is pretty fast relative to the walk. He has to do this fluently without losing the desire to step forward and while remaining supple and balanced enough to keep the forward feeling contact. If the canter is on the forehand, he is pulling himself along and it will be very difficult for him to take the weight onto the hind quarters and to step forward into the walk without losing his balance, tensing and resisting.

The key is to get a canter where the steps are short and engaged and the contact is quite light. It is best to develop this in small circles and then to ask for the first transitions to walk when facing a wall either on the straight section of a figure-of-eight or as you return to the wall from a small circle. Make a series of half-halts; no jamming on of the aids. Be sure to make the

outside rein the dominant one. At first a few steps of trot are not a problem, but it is important to keep an elastic forward-feeling contact, and to avoid tension and tightening.

At first, too, walk for as long as it takes to get him relaxed, and strike off onto the same leg. When after a while he can do this well, progress to being able to position him clearly towards a new leading leg and striking off on it.

In the upward transition, most horses will be able to pull themselves forward, leaning on the hands and taking some trot strides. The problem is that it will then be difficult to be balanced in the canter; they will be on their forehand, heavy in the hand, or resisting the contact.

In order to earn higher marks from the judges —to arrive into a better canter and to develop the Training Scales—you want the horse to spring off into the canter. Aim for him to thrust off from the walk with his hind quarters; to have an upward tendency with his shoulders; and to be light in your hands.

I like to teach this transition out of a small circle in the walk; then the horse is already in an inside flexion and the rider can be light with the inside rein and not block the forward thrust of the inside hind leg. The horse can be made more active with the rider's inside leg without the tendency to anticipate and tighten as on a straight line.

EXERCISES

Ride a squarish 10- to 15-metre circle in canter off the longside similar to the exercise described for the halt. Apply a series of half-halts when at right angles to the longside and establish the walk. Position the horse, and strike off into a 10- to 15-metre circle in the other direction. Facing the longside, especially if there is a fence or wall behind it, will stop the horse from running on when you ask for the first transition, and the small circles will help to engage him to make the transition more easily.

Often the horse will not relax in the walk and/or he may tighten against being positioned towards the new leading leg. To help this if starting on the left lead—as soon as the horse walks, leg-yield him to the left. This will help to establish the positioning for the right strike off and to encourage him to relax through his back.

Check List

Prepare for the downward transition with a series of half-halts.

Stretch up and make sure you neither lean back or forward in the transitions.

The dominant aid in the downward transition is the outside rein. Any pull back on the inside rein will block the hind leg.

Don't ask for the upward transition until he is relaxed, walking and accepting the new positioning—even if it means losing the odd mark for walking too far.

Make sure you are positioned towards the new leading leg (weight and turning shoulders in particular).

Pat him when he does it well, this is a movement that can create much tension.

Opposite is a series showing the simple change with a horse more advanced in his training and finding it much easier to engage and keep balanced than the chestnut on the previous pages.

REIN-BACK

The horse steps back, engaging his hind legs, taking more weight on the quarters, keeping a good rhythm, remaining supple, taking a consistent contact and keeping straight.

You can make a horse rein back by pulling on the reins. The problem is that it is sore on his mouth, so he usually resists and shortens his neck to try and avoid the pain, and as the hind legs cannot engage, they are dragged back and the horse hollows.

It is contrary to instinct, but for a good rein-back the dominant aids are the legs.

I like to start on the ground, with or without a rider in the saddle. I use my voice to say 'baaack' and push the horse back with my hand on his chest. When he understands that 'baaaack' means reverse, the rider can take over progressively, first with the trainer still on the ground, then, as this works, on his own.

First establish a good, balanced halt. Take your time: a little softening with the reins, then a non-allowing feel on the reins when taking your legs back and applying them well behind the girth (in this position there is no confusion with the forward driving aids). The horse will want to go forward, but the non-allowing rein aids stop him and your voice telling him 'baack' should give him the message to reverse. One step is enough to give him a big reward: a pat or even a carrot; and then over days and weeks gradually ask for more.

The rein-back. The rider is not pulling the reins back like so many riders, just not allowing with them and giving the main aid with her legs, which are being applied well back..

EXERCISES

If he tends to tighten and block against your aids, do a few steps of a turn on the forehand before asking for a rein-back.

Check List

Only ask for a rein-back when he is relaxed and soft in the halt.

Lighten your weight in the saddle by putting more weight into both stirrups.

Keep an even pressure in the reins. A stronger pull in one rein will result in the quarters drifting to the opposite side – the most common cause of crooked rein backs.

Make sure that you are not pulling him back. If necessary, check by resting your elbows on your waist before and during the rein-back (no way you can pull back then!)

LEG YIELD

Turning around the forehand is good preparation for leg-yield. The horse should have learnt to step away from your leg and you should have learnt about the importance of the outside rein. In the leg-yield the horse is kept straight, except for a slight flexion away from direction of movement. The weight is put into the stirrup of the leg on the same side as the flexion, and this leg is used close to the girth to encourage the horse to step sideways. The outside rein controls the

Leg-yielding to the left showing good crossing (left picture), Leg-yielding to the right (above) at an earlier stage in the training. When teaching the leg-yield it is best to keep the straightness with just that slight flexion at the poll away from the direction of the movement, together with the rhythm, suppleness and contact, and not ask for much crossing over.

bend, keeping the horse straight and the leg on the same side is supportive to stop the quarters getting ahead, but not active, otherwise it is a contrary aid to the driving leg. The horse is kept just about parallel to the longside, but, if anything, with the shoulders slightly ahead. If the quarters lead this will block the impulsion.

As in all the movements, the important point is to keep the Scales. Even if the horse steps sideways, speeds up, slows down, tightens, or resists, the main value of the movement as a training exercise will be lost.

Watch out for a big bend in the neck; pushing him over with the inside rein; collapsing your position, all of which will make it much more difficult for the horse to swing across in an easy, fluent rhythm.

Leg-yield can be done in walk and trot. Start with walk, progress to rising trot, and eventually, to sitting trot (as soon as you lose the swing and suppleness in the back, revert to rising trot).

EXERCISES

In the walk take an inside track from the short side. Put his head towards a wall or fence at about an angle of 45 degrees. Then apply the aids for leg-yield—flexion, inside leg, outside rein. This is difficult. He will try to change the angle, to just bend his neck, tighten, speed up, slow down. You have to react to keep the aims of the leg-yield and to pat and reward him when he does well. At first be satisfied with a few strides then progressively ask for more and start to do this exercise in trot, perhaps with less angle at first.

Come down the centre line and leg yield to the long side. You have two options according to your horse's strengths and weaknesses. If the horse is finding it difficult to cross over, come down the centre line and from the left rein leg-yield to the right. If he is finding it difficult to keep straight, from the left rein it is better to leg yield to the left.

Check List

Keeping your upright position is very important. Stretch up and put your weight into the inside stirrup.

The dominant aids are the inside leg and outside hand.

Keep the impulsion. Don't let him slow down or lose any of the other Scales.

Check that he keeps straight and does not fall onto the outside shoulder.

Above and opposite. The walk-pirouette showing the preparation with the positioning of the horse, then the turning encouraged by the rider drawing back and using actively the outside leg. The rider is staying in a good balance over the centre of the horse.

LARGE WALK PIROUETTE

This is a turn around the hind quarters and is more advanced than the turn around the forehand, because to do it well, the horse has to take weight back onto the quarters. In the tests it is done from the walk, and the horse needs to be shortening his walk steps, transferring the weight backwards as he comes into the pirouette.

The rider asks for a flexion in the direction of the movement; for a bend around his inside leg; for the turn off the track with his outside leg; and for control of the speed and bend with his outside rein. It is very important for the horse to keep the rhythm of the walk. This means that his hind legs must keep marching and describing a small circle. If one of them sticks to the ground it is considered a serious fault, so make the circle big enough to prevent this from happening and keep him active with your inside leg.

In the large walk pirouette the horse will end up off the track, hopefully only about a metre, and he should return on a straight line, no sideways steps.

EXERCISES

Start by riding a small half-circle from the long side and returning to the track on a steep diagonal. Gradually make the half-circle smaller and smaller until it turns into a large walk pirouette.

You can do the walk pirouette out of a halt or even a rein-back, which will encourage you to ride forwards and not hold back with the reins.

Check List

Aim to be ahead of the movement in the turn, as it takes a real positive effort for the rider to stay upright with the weight in the inside stirrup. Most find their seat drifting to the outside and start pushing with a collapsed seat.

Resist using the inside rein to direct the horse around as this blocks the inside hind leg.

Prepare well, so that the horse is taking the weight back, not pulling, and is flexed and soft to the inside before starting to turn.

SHOUDER-IN

Shoulder-in is, as its name implies, a matter of bringing the shoulders in off the track. To do this demands collection, as the inside hind has to step forward and under the body. If the inside hind leg steps sideways only, there will be no bend around the rider's inside leg, and no collecting effect, so it will be leg yielding. Some riders let the quarters drift out rather than bringing the shoulders in. This usually happens when the horse makes a big angle with the track when it is impossible to be supple enough to do shoulder-in. So the first things when learning shoulder-in are:

• Start in the walk when you have time to think about getting the shoulders in and not quarters out.

The shoulder-in showing the rider in a good position, her shoulders turned with those of the horse and with positive use of the outside rein. The horse is at a good angle, with the inside hind stepping into the tracks of the outside fore.

- Progress to the trot and ask for only a tiny angle off the track, known as 'shoulder-fore'. Note this is more difficult to achieve than the big angle of leg yielding.

- Keep the horse almost straight, with only a slight flexion at the poll, by using a softening inside rein but not a pulling one or one that asks for a bend in the neck.

- The dominant aids are the inside leg close to the girth and the outside rein which stops the horse from going forward, controls any bend in the neck and helps to keep the horse balanced

- The outside leg is supportive and helps to keep up the impulsion.
- The rider's position is very important - no pushing sideways, stay upright, put your weight into the inside stirrup and seat bone and turn your shoulders to help the horse turn his shoulders in off the track.

- Keep the rhythm: don't let the horse slow down.

Make it second nature to do all this in shoulder-fore, and increase the angle little by little, but never to more than 30 degrees.

Be satisfied with a relatively short distance of shoulder-in (no more than 20 metres), as it is a demanding exercise. If you run into problems and the horse starts to slow down and resist, ride out of it into a smallish circle, restore the Training Scales, and then back into the shoulder-in at the end of the circle.

EXERCISES

Ride a small circle—8 to 10 metres in diameter—when you should be using the same aids as for the shoulder-in. All you need to do is to increase the strength of your inside leg and outside rein aids as you reach the longside to go into shoulder-in.

Ride for 20 metres or so in leg-yield down one longside, then after the shortside ride for 20 metres of so in shoulder-in. Clearly understand the difference.

Check List

Bring the horse's shoulders in through use of your inside leg, outside rein and turning your shoulders.

Keep the neck almost straight: just a slight flexion at the poll.

Make sure you are stretching up and that your weight is to the inside.

Start with shoulder-fore and only progress to shoulder-in when you can keep the Training Scales in the shoulder-fore.

CHAPTER 9
THE TEST

A key aspect of test riding is preparation in all its aspects. To prepare a horse for a test you need to think about:

- Long-term preparation over months or even years so that the horse is strong enough and trained to a high enough standard to be able do the movements in the test.
- Medium-term preparations at home so that the horse can work to the best of his ability in a particular test
- Immediate preparations on the day of the test, especially with the all important riding-in and preparing in the test for each and every movement.

LONG TERM PREPARATIONS

This is the training we have been discussing in the book up to this chapter. Remember that a dressage competition is a 'test' of training. A dressage competition does not help to bring your horse on to a higher level as it does in eventing and show jumping. Rather in dressage it is best to be training at home to a higher level than the one in which you are prepared to face the judges. You will almost always have to sacrifice the Scales if you ask the horse in a test for movements that are at the limit of his current training: that he has only just enough strength and training to be able to do.

> **Check Point**
> Enter tests in which you can do all the movements easily at home.

PREPARATION FOR A COMPETITION

Start by practising a group of the movements from the test during your normal training at home. When they work well, run through the whole test. If you are not lucky enough to have

Practising the test at home. It is important to teach the horse to be relaxed in a halt when you have to salute. This rider is showing a clear salute and not just bobbing her head.

a work area, mark out an arena on the grass with poles and buckets). Note the mistakes. Think about how you are going to improve them. Work on them in some of the following training sessions and then run through the test again.

You do not always need your horse for these preparations, as 'imaging' is a great aid. Close your eyes and ride through the test in your mind, including all the preparations, and with your horse going well, so well that he would be earning 8s and 9s. If you do this mental practice and include faults it is likely you will ride for those same faults in the test. So think through the best possible test.

Check List

Learn the test.

Run through sections of the movements from it.

Run through the test.

Use mental imaging.

PREPARATION ON THE DAY

Getting to the show on time; knowing what you have to do to be ready to perform: reporting to secretary and steward; tacking up; wearing appropriate clothes and getting your horse into his gear, are very important. Make a plan beforehand as to what, and at what time, you will deal with them. It is, however, the riding-in that has the biggest impact on how well you do in the arena.

The riding-in includes you as well as the horse. Nerves tend to tighten your muscles and make you want to do everything faster. This is soon conveyed to the horse who does the same. So start by thinking about yourself. As long as your horse is relaxed enough, cross your stirrups and go back to the check list at the beginning of the book (pages 4–11). When you feel upright, stretched, balanced and supple you can start to think about the horse. Many riders do some stretching exercises and mental preparation before getting on the horse.

At Pony Club competitions shows there are tack checks, and it is important to know what you and the horse are allowed to wear. This rider is borrowing the correct equipment from another rider.

Learning the test really well is very important, but this is leaving it rather late even for a check over! Standing still does not help the suppleness before a test.

With your horse the first focus is on the Scales. You have to aim to get him going in a rhythm, to be supple and relaxed, and taking a consistent contact. If he is one of those who are full of high spirits or nervous tension at a show you need to find a way of riding-in that avoids getting into battles or wearing him out. Usually the best way is to have an early session long before the test, so that you can give him a rest before the real riding-in. You might lunge him, take him for a hack, give him a long canter in the forward seat or focus on getting him to stretch and relax in non-demanding work. The important thing is to avoid confrontation: to get

Riding-in in a low rounded outline helps to get the horse working over the back, relaxed and supple.

Work out a plan for your riding-in so that you do not move around aimlessly but include the work that develops the Scales best for you and your horse. This might be a mixture of serpentines, trot/canter/trot transitions, variations between medium and working paces, counter-canter, figures-of-eight etc, or you might focus almost entirely on, say, spiralling circles. Plan a programme so that you ask for the simple things first, then build towards those exercises like trot/walk/trot or trot to halt, and simple changes that need more engagement.

The lazy horse will need plenty of transitions to make him more sensitive; lots of variety to the work to keep him alert; and more straight lines than small circles to encourage him to think forwards. The tense forward-going horse needs above all to be settled into a constant, steady rhythm. Use plenty of circles and serpentines. Avoid straight lines, and only introduce the medium strides towards the end of the riding-in when he is more relaxed. At all costs do not let him speed up. Use your voice to soothe him.

Remember that the riding-in is the time to develop the best in your horse. It is not the time to try and tackle one of his major faults or to make a weak movement better: leave that for the training sessions at home. You want to get him working for you and showing off his good points.

Some riders like to practise all the movements required in the test, and although an increasing number spend most of their time working on the way of going—the Scales—rather than the movements, you have to decide on the programme that you feel happy with. Remember that keep-

him relaxed and listening to you through a thoughtful approach that is understanding of the reasons for his tension.

Work out at home the approximate time it takes to get your horse going at his best: that is working with rhythm, suppleness, a consistent forward feeling contact and ready to do the movements in the test. Add a few minutes more for removing the boots, giving him a last minute brush over and for plenty of short breaks when he is allowed to stretch but kept active in the walk or trot.

ing the Scales in the test will earn you most marks, and that if you do keep them, all the movements will be easier to achieve. It is not the other way around.

Give your horse plenty of breaks when he can stretch, otherwise his muscles are likely to get tired and painful and he will start to resist. Breaks also give you time to think about your position again. They are not opportunities for you to lose your focus and start gossiping! Keep your horse active and supple, so no standing around or dawdling walks, otherwise your work up to that time will have been wasted.

Check List

Plan your day to cover everything that has to be done and at what time.

Plan your riding-in, both the timing and the content.

Concentrate on developing the Training Scales.

Gradually build up to the most difficult movements in your test.

Avoid problem areas and get yourself and your horse focused, relaxed and alert.

It helps a lot to have a trainer on the ground who can check if you are in the best possible position and if the horse is going in a good way.

DRESSAGE AND THE PONY CLUB

Dressage has become an increasingly important part of Pony Club activities over the past decade. The highlight of the year is the Pony Club Championships in August. There is show jumping and eventing as well as dressage: each and everybody competing having qualified at the Area Inter-Branch competitions.

The Dressage Championship is the most difficult of the 15 Pony Club dressage tests and you have to be well on the way to becoming a Dressage Rider to score high percentages. There are many difficult transitions, simple changes, medium trots and canters, so it is a good test of a champion.

INTER BRANCH COMPETITIONS

At the Area Inter-Branch Competitions the tests are easier, and it is a great goal for riders to be selected for a team and to represent their Branch. Inter-Branch competitions now have three levels: Novice, Intermediate and Open, all leading to Championships. Your Branch can select you as a team member or an individual.

EASY STARTERS

The great thing about the Pony Club is that in all the different sports there is a very easy entry level. At the other end of the spectrum from the Championships, the tests are so easy that you only have to do walk and trot. This a great start for those who are trying out some dressage—especially if they are very young.

RIDING TO MUSIC

Variations of the dressage test are used for some Pony Club competitions, and one that is demanding but fun to do is dressage to music. This tests your artistic flair and your ability to find and record music that suits your horse and to which his hoofbeats are in time. There are certain movements that have to be carried out and it is up to the rider to design a choreography that includes them and works well with the music. The marks in these tests are *technical ones* for the various dressage movements that have to be included, and

The 2005 and 2006 winner of the Individual ride-off at the Pony Club Championships, Olivia Kuropatwa, training at home.

artistic ones for:

1. Rhythm, Energy and Elasticity,
2. Harmony between rider and horse,
3. Choreography. Use of arena. Inventiveness, and
4. Music and interpretation of the music.

Dressage to music is a real challenge, but great fun; horse and rider seem to relax more when they are following a beat.

FOCUS ON THE RIDER

As this book has emphasised so often: until the rider can sit in balance with the horse he cannot expect his horse to go well. In order to encourage riders to put the work in to improving their positions, dressage competitions have been introduced where the tests focus on the position of the rider and the influence he/she has over the horse. There is a special score sheet that gives

For the second year running the V.W.H. Pony Club were the dressage team winners at the Pony Club Championships. From left to right: Tom McEwen, Pippa Hutton, Olivia Kuropatwa, and Charlie Hutton. Tom and Olivia have been guinea pigs for the photos in this book.

marks just for the way the rider sits, his balance and his influence over the horse.

TRAINING

Most Pony Club Branches provide very good dressage training at their rallies and camps. Many international champions who began their riding with the Pony Club are keen to go back and give the next generation some of the help from which they benefited all those years ago!

CENTRE MEMBERSHIP

As well as the opportunities mentioned above for Pony Club Branch Members a recent and very successful development is Pony Club Centre Membership. This is based on over 400 affiliated Riding Schools—so you do not need your own horse in order to join. Centre Members have plenty of opportunities to compete in dressage. There are Dressage to Music competitions, Inter-Centre Combined Training, Centre League Competitions, and Video Dressage Competitions where you can compete against different centres without having to travel.

The Pony Club offers everybody, whether you have a horse or not, a chance to try out dressage: so if you are not already on the road towards becoming a Dressage Rider, go to it and give it a whirl with the Pony Club!

GLOSSARY

There are plenty of terms in dressage that cause lots of confusion. The judges put them on the score sheets and riders become confused. A problem is that dressage developed in Germany and France and there are no direct translations for many of the words they use for this sport. Some English words have been used in a way that you would not find in the dictionary, so to help you understand what the judges and trainers are talking about, the following are the main terms you will come across, with an explanation alongside.

Above the bit The horse lifts his head and neck and hollows his back. Usually this is due to resistance but can be a loss of balance.

Behind the bit The horse does not want to take the contact and avoids doing so by bringing his head back closer to his chest. This is a serious fault.

Behind the vertical The vertical is a line running from the poll down to the ground. Ideally, the horse's head should be on or just in front of it. Falling behind the vertical is not a serious fault if it is only for a short time, nor if the rider still has a light elastic contact in his hands. It is serious when the horse drops behind the bit and avoids the contact.

Between the leg and hand This is when the rider can use his legs to ride the horse forward into a contact that is felt in his hands. The horse is contained between the legs and hands. It is the contact we are looking for in the Scales of Training.

Broken neck Ideally there should be a continuous arch to the neck from the withers to the poll, but in this case the horse bends his neck more extremely at the third or fourth vertebra so the poll is no longer the highest point.

Bend Bend is a continuous curve in the horse's body from his hind quarters to his head.

Cadence There is a pronounced beat to the rhythm that comes from finding the best tempo for the horse in question, keeping a good balance and having plenty of impulsion.

Change the rein Changing the direction from clockwise (right rein) to anti-clockwise (left rein), or vice-versa.

Contact Contact is felt in the hands as a consistent, elastic, soft contact with the bit. It is made not by the hands, but by the legs (and seat) encouraging the hind legs to thrust forward and the momentum thus created going through the back and neck to the mouth and being felt in the hands.

Counter-canter Normally the leading leg is on the inside of a turn or circle, but in counter-canter it is the outside foreleg that leads.

Disunited The horse leads with a different leg in front from behind. This is uncomfortable for the rider and unbalancing for the horse.

Elasticity The horse can stretch and contract his muscles smoothly to give an impression of springiness and stretchiness.

Expression The movement is expressive, showing flamboyance, spring and elasticity rather than being flat and dull. This is good as long as it is produced through good training and natural ability and not because the horse is tense and nervous.

Flexion The horse keeps the neck straight but turns

his head slightly at the poll and jaw.

Impulsion This is the contained power of the horse enabling him to show off longer strides in extensions and higher ones in collection. It is produced by thrust from the hind legs. It can be contained only when the muscles work freely and do not tighten and block the passage of the power to the bit, and when the horse accepts the contact and does not try to speed up.

Inside This is the direction in which the horse is bent or flexed.

Irregular The horse loses the correct rhythm to the pace i.e. two-time walk, four-time canter.

Leaning The horse uses the reins to give him support, taking a strong contact and usually falling onto his forehand.

On the forehand Much of the novice horse's weight falls onto the shoulders, neck and head. His movement is cumbersome and restricted. The aim of dressage is to make the horse more balanced by training him to transfer more and more of the weight onto the hind quarters. Then the forehand becomes freer and more mobile.

Outline/frame The silhouette of the horse along the top line from the poll to the hind quarters.

Over-tracking The hind foot steps in front of the hoof print left by the forefoot on that same side.

Pacing This is a serious fault in the walk when the foreleg and hind leg on the same side move parallel to each other in a two-time rhythm. The correct four-time rhythm has been lost.

Rhythm This is the sequence of footfalls for each pace. When it is regular it is correct.

Round The outline tends towards being rounded with an arched neck and the hind quarters stepping forward under the horse's body.

Self-carriage The horse carries itself in a balanced and unconstrained way, taking a light elastic contact but not relying on the reins for support. The horse can be in self-carriage when he is stretching long and low, as well as when he is in a classical position with his head just in front of the vertical.

Short in the neck The neck is compressed backwards towards the withers and chest so the arched stretching of the neck is lost. It is usually due to the rider holding the horse with a backward feeling in the hands.

Swinging through back The horse's back muscles work freely, contracting and relaxing without any tightness and tension. This enables the thrust from the hind legs to flow through the back to produce a stretchiness to the contact. If the contact is eased the horse will stretch his head and neck forward and down.

Square halt A balanced halt when the two forelegs are parallel as are the hind legs. The weight is shared evenly.

Step This is the movement of one leg.

Stride This is the movement of the four legs in sequence, i.e. four steps.

Tempo This is the speed of the rhythm of the walk, trot or canter.

Throughness This is the responsiveness of the horse to the aids and the ability to allow the aids to flow through his entire body. Any resistance, tightness, stiffness, will block the throughness and stop the horse responding correctly.

Tilting The horse does not flex at the poll when asked to turn his head. Instead he brings his mouth in and up so that one ear is lower than the other. The head is no longer vertical

Tracking up The horse steps with his hind feet into the hoof prints of the corresponding forefeet.

Uneven The steps are not of equal length

Unlevel The steps are not of equal height so the horse does not take equal weight on them.

Working from behind The hind legs start the movement, helping to generate impulsion. The horse does not pull himself along by moving the fore legs first.

INDEX

Page numbers in **bold** refer to illustrations